Prego

16
17
18

Descartes

The Quick Gourmet Cookbook

Other books by Ceil Dyer

The Back to Cooking Cookbook

The Breakfast Cookbook

The Freezer Cookbook

Hamburgers Plain and Fancy

The Plan-Ahead Cookbook

The Quick and Easy Electric Skillet Cookbook

The Sweet Taste of Success

THE QUICK GOURMET COOKBOOK

EASY AND ELEGANT WAYS TO PREPARE

LUNCHEONS, SUPPERS, AND DINNERS

by Ceil Dyer

HAWTHORN BOOKS, INC., Publishers, NEW YORK

Contents

Introduction

Between *haute cuisine* and commercially prepared, so-called convenience foods, there is a very satisfactory and nutritious middle road to pleasurable dining. Certainly, great French cooking can be a worthy avocation, but it also takes time, and except for rare occasions, very few of us have either the leisure or the inclination these days to spend hours in the kitchen. There is an alternative to elaborate, time-consuming methods of preparing meals, and it has nothing to do with TV dinners, canned soups, dehydrated sauces, bottled salad dressing, frozen vegetables in frozen sauce, or any other of these bland, tasteless, overpriced concoctions. It is nothing more than the simple science and pleasant art of preparing tasteful meals from basic ingredients without fanfare or fuss. Its rules are simple, and its skills are few. It's only a matter of knowing and doing.

First, dismiss the idea that all great cuisines are based on slowly cooked foods. It's simply not true, as anyone who knows the preparation time for most fine Chinese dishes will enthusiastically testify.

Second, forget the old-fashioned American blue-plate notion that every meal except breakfast must consist of meat, potatoes, vegetables, a salad, and dessert. There's a whole world of delicious menus that are easier and quicker to prepare.

Next, expand your quick-cooking repertoire with a knowledge of herbs and spices. Learn the quick tricks of garnishes, and become acquainted with the professional chef's way with sauce.

Lastly, you can change your outdated pattern of cooking every meal from scratch by making full use of your refrigerator and freezer. Make double portions of any rice or pasta dish—one to eat and one to freeze—and always cook more vegetables than you plan to serve, using the extras for the next day's salad or hors d'oeuvre. Prepare stock once a week (or once a month) to have on hand for quick-cooking but absolutely superb soups, sauces, and stews. (While you're at it, cook a chicken or a brisket of beef in the same pot for the next day's easy meal.) The recipes for these easily prepared but superb stocks are on pages 22–24.

You'll find no recipe in this book that takes more than its fair share of your short kitchen time, and none of the recipes is difficult to prepare. The recipes are presented with some of the quick-cooking ideas and tricks of the trade that I have gathered from good cooks and professional chefs from all over the globe. The cooking methods are simple, and the dishes you will create will delight a generation that is short on time but too knowledgeable and sophisticated to settle for commercially packaged trite and dull foods. In short, this is a book that wants you to hurry out of the kitchen and then relax and enjoy a leisurely meal that is both delectable and nourishing.

1

Cocktail-Hour "Go-Withs"

Appetizers should never be just an afterthought—an extra something to serve with drinks before the meal—but an important part of the meal itself. Whether they replace a formal first course or are served as little hot or cold morsels to whet the appetite, they are part of the total menu.

An assortment of made-ahead fresh-vegetable appetizers—*hors d'oeuvres variés*—can replace a salad that would otherwise accompany or follow the main-course dish. An authentic Italian antipasto set out buffet-style is all that is needed before that one great pasta dish, and an interesting and varied assortment of canapés may precede a hot, thick soup which, with dessert, can add up to a truly memorable meal.

On the other hand, a hearty peasant-style *osso buco* calls for nothing more complicated than one quick-to-assemble curtain raiser such as a bowl of fresh figs wrapped in paper-thin slices of prosciutto. Such classic French fare as *boeuf bourguignonne* or Marseilles bouillabaisse should never be preceded by anything more complicated than *salade de champignons* (sliced fresh mushrooms, lemon juice, oil, parsley, and chives) and perhaps one or two hot little bite-size cheese or seafood tarts to complement a first glass of the same wine that will accompany these one-dish main courses.

In each case the total menu is more harmonious, and there's less work involved. Yet the end results add up to more pleasurable dining and a more leisurely meal. Now, what more could you ask?

1

In this first chapter you'll find a goodly assortment of appetizers, hors d'oeuvres, or "go-withs"—call them what you will—that can be served separately before a hearty lunch or dinner or in any number of combinations as part of a well-balanced menu. Each one can be classified under quick cooking, and almost all can be made ahead of time—or at least made ready for a few last minutes of assembling or baking.

Vegetables

Vegetable appetizers have much to recommend them. They are low-calorie, can be utterly delicious, and since they must be made ahead to chill before serving, are good when planning quick-to-the-table meals.

Curtain Raisers

Spear pitted black or green olives with crisp carrot sticks.

Brush thin slices of raw turnip with lemon juice. Spread with soft cheddar cheese.

Mash sardines that are packed in mustard sauce. Season with Worcestershire, Tabasco, black pepper, and salt. Stuff large raw mushroom caps with mixture.

Dip cold cooked asparagus in mayonnaise. Wrap in paper-thin slices of prosciutto or baked Virginia ham. Secure with cocktail picks.

Cut small peeled cucumbers into strips. Wrap each strip in a thin slice of smoked salmon, and secure with cocktail picks.

Scoop out the centers of small cooked and chilled brussels sprouts, and fill with equal parts of blue cheese and cream cheese thinned with a little Cognac or other good brandy.

Spread thin slices of dried beef with cream cheese. Cover with chopped watercress and chives. Roll up, and secure with cocktail picks.

Scoop out the center of small boiled and chilled white onions. Fill with Smithfield ham spread. Press a small pimiento-stuffed olive into the center.

Marinate thin strips of raw zucchini in French dressing. Drain. Wrap an anchovy fillet around each, and secure with cocktail picks.

Stuffed Vegetables

Plain carrot sticks and celery curls may go begging, but not vegetables that have been stuffed with a savory filling.

CHEESE-STUFFED CHERRY TOMATOES

24 small cherry tomatoes
Salt
½ pound sharp cheddar cheese, grated
3 ounces cream cheese
2 tablespoons Cognac or other good brandy

1 small jar pimiento-stuffed green olives, drained and finely chopped
2 or 3 dashes Tabasco sauce
½ cup minced parsley

Cut a thin slice from the stem end of each tomato. With a small spoon scoop out the center pulp. (You may reserve pulp for another use.) Sprinkle the inside of each tomato with salt, and invert on paper toweling to drain for 10 to 15 minutes.

Combine cheddar cheese, cream cheese, and Cognac. Blend until smooth, then add chopped olives and Tabasco sauce.

Fill tomatoes with mixture, and sprinkle with parsley.

PÂTÉ-STUFFED ONIONS

12 to 14 small white onions, peeled
3 tablespoons butter
1 pound chicken livers
½ teaspoon curry powder

½ teaspoon salt
¼ teaspoon pepper
Dry sherry

Place onions in a saucepan with salted water to cover. Let simmer until tender but not mushy. Drain. With a small sharp knife scoop out the center of each onion. Set shells aside, and chop scooped-out centers.

Melt the butter in a skillet. Add the chopped onion, chicken livers, curry powder, and salt and pepper. Stir over moderate heat until livers are cooked but not browned.

Transfer to a mixing bowl, and mash with a fork until smooth, adding sufficient sherry to make a smooth thick paste.

Stuff onion shells with mixture, and refrigerate 3 to 4 hours before serving.

ROQUEFORT-STUFFED MUSHROOMS

¼ pound Roquefort cheese	½ teaspoon Worcestershire sauce
6 ounces cream cheese	1½ pounds large mushrooms
¼ cup mayonnaise	½ cup minced parsley
1 teaspoon lemon juice	

Mash Roquefort cheese with cream cheese. Beat in mayonnaise, lemon juice, and Worcestershire sauce.

Remove stems from mushrooms, and reserve for another use. Fill mushroom caps with cheese mixture, mounding it high. Sprinkle with parsley.

Serves 6 to 8.

CUCUMBERS STUFFED WITH SHRIMP

4 medium cucumbers	2 or 3 dashes Tabasco sauce
1 pound cooked shrimp, shelled and deveined	2 tablespoons Cognac or other good brandy
1 3-ounce package cream cheese at room temperature	Salt
	Freshly ground black pepper
1 teaspoon Dijon mustard	Cocktail rye bread, thinly sliced

Peel cucumbers with a fluted vegetable knife. Remove centers with an apple corer.

Chop shrimp very fine. Place in mixing bowl, and add cream cheese, mustard, Tabasco, Cognac, and salt and pepper. Blend well.

Stuff cucumbers with mixture, and refrigerate until well chilled. Cut into thick slices, and serve on small thin rounds of rye bread.

Vegetable "Go-Withs"

These may be served separately or as one of the dishes in a selection of appetizers.

SALADE DE CHAMPIGNONS
(Fresh Mushroom Salad Appetizer)

1½ pounds firm large white mushrooms
2 tablespoons lemon juice
4 tablespoons salad oil
6 anchovy fillets, drained and chopped
2 tablespoons minced chives
2 tablespoons minced parsley
Salt to taste
Freshly ground black pepper to taste
Small crisp leaves of Bibb lettuce

Wash mushrooms, pat dry, and cut off tough stem ends. Chop coarsely, and place in a nonmetal bowl. Add remaining ingredients except lettuce, and toss lightly to blend.

Let stand 30 to 45 minutes, then pour off excess liquid.

Spoon small mounds of mixture onto small crisp leaves of Bibb lettuce. Serve on small plates, and provide cocktail forks.

Or spoon onto small leaves of lettuce, and roll up and secure with cocktail picks. Serve as finger food, and provide cocktail napkins for holding.

Serves 4 to 6.

BRANDIED MUSHROOMS AND BLACK OLIVES

1 pound small button mushrooms
3 tablespoons oil
1 tablespoon lemon juice
1 clove garlic, peeled
Salt
Freshly ground black pepper
1 small can pitted black olives, drained
¼ cup Cognac or other good brandy

Place mushrooms, oil, lemon juice, and garlic in a small saucepan, and cook, stirring often, over moderate heat for 8 to 10 minutes.

Pour into a nonmetal bowl, and sprinkle lightly with salt and pepper. Add olives and Cognac.

Refrigerate 6 hours or longer. Drain, and serve with cocktail picks for spearing.

Serves 6 to 8.

ARTICHOKE HEARTS PIQUANT

¼ cup olive oil
1 clove garlic, peeled and cut in half
2 9-ounce packages frozen artichoke hearts
1 small jar button mushrooms, drained

2 tablespoons fresh lemon juice
6 anchovy fillets, drained and chopped
Freshly ground black pepper
Salt

Heat the oil with the garlic in a large skillet. Add the frozen artichoke hearts, and cook over low heat until defrosted and hot. Remove garlic, and stir in mushrooms.

Transfer to a nonmetal bowl, and add lemon juice and anchovy fillets. Toss lightly, and season generously with pepper. Taste, and add salt if desired.

Cover and refrigerate until chilled.

Drain off excess liquid. Serve on small plates, and provide cocktail forks.

Serves 4 to 6.

FLAGEOLETS VINAIGRETTE

2 1-pound jars or cans flageolets (imported small white kidney beans)
1 cup salad oil
¼ cup white-wine vinegar
1 clove garlic, peeled and cut in half

1 large white onion, peeled and finely chopped
½ cup chopped ripe olives
½ teaspoon salt
¼ teaspoon freshly ground black pepper
½ cup finely chopped parsley

Drain beans, and combine with remaining ingredients. Cover and refrigerate 4 to 12 hours.

Remove garlic. Drain off excess liquid. Provide small cocktail forks, and serve on small plates.

Serves 6 to 8.

VEGETABLES VINAIGRETTE

6 to 8 small young carrots, scraped and cut into finger-length sticks

6 to 8 very small whole baby beets, peeled

1 small cauliflower, cut into flowerets

6 to 8 tiny white onions, peeled

1 9-ounce package frozen artichoke hearts

¾ cup salad oil

¼ cup white-wine vinegar

1 tablespoon salt

½ tablespoon freshly ground black pepper

½ teaspoon sugar

1 clove garlic, peeled (optional)

8 to 10 large black olives

6 to 8 cherry tomatoes

Mustard Mayonnaise (pages 7–8)

Hot Anchovy Dip (page 8)

Cook carrots, beets, cauliflower, onions, and artichokes in boiling salted water until just barely tender.

Drain. While still warm combine vegetables in a large nonmetal bowl with oil, vinegar, salt, pepper, sugar, and garlic.

Cover and let marinate in the refrigerator until well chilled.

Remove garlic. Add olives and tomatoes. Toss well.

Drain off marinade, and arrange on a large serving platter. Serve with cocktail picks and fondue forks for easy dunking into choice of cold Mustard Mayonnaise or Hot Anchovy Dip.

Serves 6 to 8.

MUSTARD MAYONNAISE

1 cup Basic Mayonnaise (pages 34–35)

1 tablespoon lemon juice

2 tablespoons Dijon or Düsseldorf mustard

½ cup sour cream

Salt

Freshly ground black pepper

Paprika

Combine Basic Mayonnaise, lemon juice, and mustard. Beat with a wire whisk until blended.

Fold in sour cream. Add salt and pepper to taste. Chill. Dust with paprika just before serving.

HOT ANCHOVY DIP

¼ pound butter
¾ cup olive oil
1 clove garlic, peeled and mashed
8 to 10 anchovy fillets, chopped

½ cup finely minced parsley
Freshly ground black pepper
Salt

Combine butter and oil in a fondue pot or chafing dish over medium flame. Add garlic and anchovy fillets. Heat to steaming. Add parsley. Season generously with pepper. Taste, and add salt if desired. Keep warm over low heat.

Let guests dunk prepared vegetables into dip before eating "hot from the pot."

ITALIAN SALAD

6 stalks celery, cut into ½-inch lengths
1 small cauliflower, trimmed and broken into flowerets
½ pound small button mushrooms
1 green pepper, seeded and cut into narrow strips
1 clove garlic, peeled
¼ cup tarragon vinegar
⅔ cup olive oil

1 small jar Sicilian black olives
1 small jar pitted green olives
1 small jar pickled onions
1 small can anchovy fillets
1 small can tuna in oil
1 small can pimientos, cut into thin strips
1 small jar capers
Salt
Pepper

Fill a large saucepan with salted water, and bring to a full boil. Add celery, cauliflower, mushrooms, green pepper, and garlic. Let water come to a full boil once again, then reduce heat. Let vegetables simmer for about 5 minutes. Remove garlic clove. Drain and cool.

Place in a large salad bowl. Add remaining ingredients except for salt and pepper, and toss well.

Season to taste with salt and pepper. Cover and place in the refrigerator 6 or more hours.

Let stand at room temperature 30 to 45 minutes. This salad tastes better if served cool but not really cold. Drain off excess liquid before serving.

This is a beautiful-to-look-at mixture, so bring the bowl in where it can be admired before ladling portions onto small plates. Be sure to provide small forks.

Serves 10 to 12.

Fruit

Wash a pint of fresh Bing cherries. Place in a nonmetal bowl, and add a cup of dry white wine. Refrigerate 6 hours or longer. Drain just before serving.

Peel and cut a large fresh pineapple into bite-size wedges. Place in a nonmetal bowl, and add a cup of gin and 2 tablespoons chopped chives. Toss to blend. Refrigerate 6 hours or longer. Drain just before serving.

Brush slices of crisp tart apples with lemon juice. Cream equal parts Roquefort cheese and cream cheese with sufficient Cognac to make a smooth spread. Cover apple slices with mixture mounded high, and sprinkle with chives.

Wrap peeled whole figs in paper-thin slices of prosciutto ham, and secure with cocktail picks.

Marinate fresh pineapple chunks in Jamaican rum 6 hours or overnight. Drain. Wrap each cube in a strip of bacon. Broil until bacon is crisp.

Peel and cut ripe but firm peaches into bite-size chunks. Marinate in French dressing (made with 3 parts oil to 1 part fresh lemon juice) for 2 to 3 hours. Drain. Sprinkle with chives, and spear each cube with a cocktail pick.

Marinate small clusters of grapes in Marsala wine 12 to 24 hours. Drain and serve with wedges of Switzerland Swiss cheese.

Antipasto

Antipasto is the traditional first course of an Italian meal, but you don't always have to serve an all-Italian meal to enjoy it. Serve it as hors d'oeuvres before any fairly light entrée, such as a casserole of noodles and cheese or a main-course dish that features fish or seafood.

The ingredients can be as simple and few or as varied and numerous as you please, but for the real thing make your selection from the classic antipasto ingredients below.

Fresh crisp salad greens (any and/or all types, dressed very lightly with just enough dressing of oil, vinegar, and garlic to cling to the leaves)

Tomato wedges

Quartered hard-cooked eggs

Radishes

Celery hearts

Sliced fresh raw mushrooms or (preferred) *funghi con aceto e olio* (mushrooms marinated in an oil and vinegar dressing and sautéed in olive oil)

Artichoke hearts (canned or bottled Italian style)

Anchovy fillets

Green olives

Olive nere all'olio (black olives cured in oil instead of brine)

Pimientos

Peperoncini all'aceto (tart little pickled green peppers)

Paper-thin slices of salami (Italian sausage), prosciutto (Italian ham), *salsiccia secca* (very dry pork sausage)

Provolone (a mild Italian cheese)
Pickled beets
Thin slices of Persian melon
Uovo di aringhe (herring roe)
Uovo di tonno (tuna-fish roe)
Chunks of tuna in oil

Canapés

The first commandment in the good cook's book of rules: Thou shall not serve soggy canapés. Start with a firm base—always toast your bread, and butter it well. The butter prevents seepage and helps keep the bread fresh.

Use an assembly-line procedure for preparing canapés. Prepare spreads and garnishes. Bring butter to room temperature. Stack three, four, or more slices of bread, and trim off crust. Repeat for as many slices as needed. Toast bread lightly on both sides. Cool. Place six or more slices of toast on a cutting board or kitchen table. Spread with soft butter. Spoon a mound of spread on each, then smooth out with a butter knife, covering each completely with spread. Cut into four finger strips, triangles, or squares. Top with any desired garnish: thin slices of pimiento, stuffed green olive slices, anchovy fillets, capers, or a sprinkling of red caviar, minced parsley, or chives. Place canapés in a long shallow pan or on a serving platter. Cover with foil or plastic wrap, and refrigerate until ready to serve.

For the cook without time canapés can be served on a do-it-yourself basis.

Pack spread in an earthenware jar or spoon into an attractive small bowl, surround with toast points, cocktail rye rounds, or crackers, and let each guest spread his own.

Notes to the Dieter

Crisp cucumber slices and carrot ovals are tasty bases for canapés.

Peel cucumbers, and cut into fairly thick slices. With a spoon scoop out a small well in the center of each. Fill and spread completely with any cheese, meat, or fish spread. Scrape large carrots and cut them Chinese-fashion at a 45° angle into thin oval slices. Keep them crisp in a bowl of ice water until ready to use. Blot thoroughly dry before spreading with any good spread.

Another great base for cheese spreads is thin slices of fresh pineapple cut into bite-size wedges. Also, and my all-time favorite—thin slices of raw turnip. Keep turnip slices crisp in a bowl of ice water into which you have squeezed the juice of 1 lemon. Blot dry before using.

Canapé Spreads and Dips

CHEESE SPREAD OR DIP

Take equal parts of soft butter at room temperature and any good soft or semisoft cheese. Blend together with sufficient liquid to make a smooth spread. The liquid: dry sherry, Cognac or other good brandy, kümmel, aquavit, gin, beer, or dry white wine.

BAVARIAN CHEESE SPREAD OR DIP

¼ pound butter
½ pound mild soft cheddar cheese

¾ cup beer
Dash cayenne pepper

Bring all ingredients to room temperature. Cream butter with cheese, then beat in beer and cayenne.

Makes about 1½ cups spread.

SHRIMP CHEESE SPREAD OR DIP

½ pound cooked shrimp, shelled and deveined
6 ounces Crema Danica or Philadelphia cream cheese

2 teaspoons Cognac or other good brandy
Salt
Freshly ground black pepper
2 tablespoons minced parsley

Chop shrimp very fine. Add cheese and Cognac. Blend well, and season lightly with salt and pepper.

Fold in parsley, or use parsley as garnish for canapés.
Makes about 1½ cups spread.

AVOCADO SPREAD OR DIP

3 medium avocados
2 teaspoons minced onion
3 hard-cooked eggs, finely
chopped

1 tablespoon lemon juice
2 tablespoons dry white wine
Salt

Cut avocados in half. Remove seed and scoop out pulp. Combine with remaining ingredients. Blend well. Use as cold canapé spread, or prepare canapés, and put under the broiler until very hot.
Makes about 1½ cups spread.

SOUTHERN HAM AND PEANUT SPREAD

¾ cup salted peanuts, chopped
very fine
1 cup minced boiled or baked
ham

Basic Mayonnaise (approximately ½ cup) (pages 34–35)

Combine peanuts and ham. Add sufficient mayonnaise to bind into a smooth spread.
Easy but delicious.
Makes about 2¼ cups spread.

SARDINE AND CHIVE SPREAD

2 cans sardines in olive oil
¼ pound sweet butter at room
temperature
3 tablespoons minced chives

1 tablespoon lemon juice
1 teaspoon salt
⅛ teaspoon cayenne pepper

Place sardines in a mixing bowl, and mash with a fork to a smooth pulp. Add the butter, and blend well. Add remaining ingredients, and beat until well blended.
Makes about 1 cup spread.

CHICKEN-LIVER AND ALMOND SPREAD

3 tablespoons butter
1 pound chicken livers
1 small white onion, minced
½ teaspoon paprika
¼ teaspoon salt

¼ teaspoon freshly ground black pepper
¼ cup Cognac or other good brandy
¾ cup butter at room temperature
½ cup finely chopped almonds

Place the 3 tablespoons butter in a saucepan over low heat. When melted, add the chicken livers, onion, paprika, and salt and pepper. Cover and cook 8 to 10 minutes. Stir occasionally.

Transfer mixture to an electric blender. Add the Cognac, and blend until smooth.

Place in a mixing bowl, add the ¾ cup butter, and blend well. Stir in chopped almonds.

Makes about 3 cups spread.

Tarts, Quiches, and Other Pastry Hors d'Oeuvres

Elegant hot hors d'oeuvres start with croustades—little bread cases—that substitute nicely for all but the finest puff pastry, and in my opinion they taste even better. They can be made ahead and then frozen until needed. What's more, the "fillings" can be made ahead, too.

CROUSTADES

24 slices very fresh white bread, thinly sliced

3 tablespoons butter at room temperature and very soft

Using a 3-inch cookie cutter, cut each slice of bread into 3-inch rounds. Spread each completely with soft butter, then fit the rounds, butter side down, into miniature muffin tins. (Tins should be about 2 inches round at the top.) Gently press and mold each slice around the bottom and sides of the tins so that they fit neatly and form little cups.

Place in a preheated 375° oven, and bake for 3 to 5 minutes or until bread is crisp but not browned.

Remove from tins and cool. If desired, refrigerate or freeze until ready to use. Frozen croustades should be filled and baked without thawing.

MINIATURE QUICHES

1 8-ounce package cream cheese at room temperature
1 tablespoon Cognac or other good brandy
1 egg yolk, lightly beaten
¼ teaspoon salt
¼ teaspoon pepper
2 or 3 dashes Tabasco sauce
¾ cup finely chopped baked or boiled ham
24 Croustades (pages 14–15)

Combine cream cheese and Cognac. Add egg yolk, salt, pepper, and Tabasco. Beat with a wire whisk until light and fluffy.

Sprinkle a little chopped ham into each croustade, and fill with cheese mixture.

Arrange filled croustades on a baking sheet. Place in a preheated 375° oven, and bake 8 to 10 minutes or until cheese puffs up.

Serve hot from the oven.

Makes 24 quiches.

CHICKEN CROUSTADES WITH SOUR CREAM

1 cup ground or very finely minced cooked chicken
1 tablespoon finely minced chives
1 tablespoon finely minced parsley
3 slices crisp cooked bacon, finely crumbled
Sour cream
Salt
Freshly ground black pepper
18 Croustades (pages 14–15)
2 tablespoons grated Parmesan cheese
2 tablespoons fine dry bread crumbs
3 tablespoons melted butter

Combine chicken, chives, parsley, and bacon. Add just enough sour cream to hold mixture together. Season with salt and pepper. Spoon into prepared croustades. Sprinkle with grated cheese, bread crumbs, and melted butter.

Bake in a preheated 400° oven until filling is bubbly hot. Serve at once.

Makes 18 croustades.

SAVORY CROUSTADES

¾ cup Major Gray chutney, drained and coarsely chopped
½ cup chopped unsalted peanuts
¼ cup white raisins
½ cup grated or finely crumbled sharp cheddar cheese
24 Croustades (pages 14–15)

Combine chutney with peanuts, raisins, and cheese. Mix well, and spoon into croustades.

Arrange on baking sheet, and place in a preheated 375° oven. Bake 8 to 10 minutes or until piping hot. Serve at once.

Makes 24 croustades.

CRABMEAT CROUSTADES

2 tablespoons butter
2 large mushrooms, finely chopped
1 tablespoon minced chives
2 tablespoons flour
1 cup milk
¼ teaspoon salt
¼ teaspoon pepper
1 egg yolk
1 tablespoon dry sherry
1 pound fresh or canned crabmeat, flaked and well picked over
24 Croustades (pages 14–15)

Melt the butter in a heavy saucepan over low heat. Add the mushrooms and chives. Sauté 1 minute. Sprinkle with flour, and cook, stirring, until no trace of flour remains.

Slowly add the milk, stirring as it is added. Season with salt and pepper, and continue to cook, stirring, until sauce begins to thicken.

Beat the egg yolk with the sherry, and quickly stir this into the sauce. Cook, stirring, until very thick. Remove from heat, and stir in crabmeat.

Cover surface directly with plastic wrap, and set aside until ready to use.

Spoon crabmeat mixture into prepared croustades. Arrange on a baking sheet in a preheated 400° oven, and bake 8 to 10 minutes or until bubbly hot. Then place directly under broiler heat for a few seconds until top is lightly browned.

Serve hot.

Makes 24 croustades.

DOUBLE CHEESE PUFFS

Cheese puffs have this to recommend them: They are made from the only easy-to-make classic French pastry dough. Besides this, they are light, airy, and truly delicious. Made ahead, they can be reheated successfully.

1 cup water
¼ pound butter, cut into small pieces
1 cup flour
5 eggs at room temperature
1 teaspoon Dijon mustard

½ teaspoon salt
½ cup grated Parmesan cheese
1 teaspoon water
½ pound Swiss cheese, cut in small cubes

Place the cup of water in a 2-quart saucepan over medium-high heat. Add the butter, and bring to a full boil. When butter has completely melted, remove pan from heat, and immediately add the flour all at once, stirring rapidly until blended. Reduce heat to low, return pan to heat, and stir vigorously until mixture leaves the sides of the pan and forms a stiff dough. Remove from heat, and add 4 of the eggs, one at a time, beating thoroughly after each addition. Beat in mustard, salt, and Parmesan cheese.

Place level teaspoons of batter on ungreased baking sheet about 1 inch apart. Brush tops with remaining egg beaten with 1 teaspoon water.

Place in a preheated 400° oven, and bake 10 minutes. Reduce heat to 325° without opening door, and continue to bake for 20 minutes. Remove from oven, and cool.

With the tip of a spoon cut a small opening in each puff, and insert a small cube of Swiss cheese. (*Puffs can be made ahead to this point. Store in plastic bags in the refrigerator until ready to bake.*)

Return filled puffs to a 350° oven, and bake a final 5 to 8 minutes. Serve hot.

Makes about 24 puffs.

Thanks to the "gourmet" frozen-food section of your handy super-market, it is no longer necessary to spend hours in the kitchen preparing puff pastry for hot hors d'oeuvres, nor is it necessary to settle for plain frozen pie crust as you may have done in the past. Instead, you can look for and usually find a package of frozen Greek *phyllo* pastry sheets that will substitute nicely for, and surpass in lightness, all but the pastry of a professional French chef.

Easy to use, they make possible hot-from-the-oven hors d'oeuvres in double-quick time.

TARTE AU FROMAGE

5 eggs
1⅓ cups light cream
⅓ pound Swiss cheese, grated
2 tablespoons grated Parmesan cheese
⅓ teaspoon salt
Dash of nutmeg
Dash of cayenne pepper
Butter
¼ pound Greek *phyllo* pastry sheets
4 tablespoons melted butter, slightly cooled

Combine eggs and cream, and beat until blended. Add cheese and seasoning.

Lightly butter a 9-inch pie pan. Line with 7 or 8 overlapping layers of *phyllo* pastry sheets, brushing each sheet first on both sides with melted butter. Keep unused pastry sheets covered with a damp cloth until ready to brush with butter. Trim edges of pastry to fit rim of pie pan, and brush with melted butter. Pour in egg mixture.

Place pie pan in a preheated 400° oven for 15 minutes. Brush exposed crust with butter, lower heat to 325°, and continue to bake until custard is firm.

Serve from the pan.

Serves 6 to 8.

ANCHOVY CHEESE SQUARES

1 2-ounce can anchovy fillets
2 eggs, beaten
½ pound ricotta cheese
2 tablespoons grated Romano cheese
1 tablespoon minced parsley
3 tablespoons butter

4 tablespoons flour
1 cup milk
¼ teaspoon pepper
½ pound Greek *phyllo* pastry sheets
¼ pound melted butter

Drain and chop anchovies.

Place eggs in a large mixing bowl, add cheeses, and beat until blended. Add parsley and anchovies.

Melt the butter in a small saucepan, add the flour, and stir until blended. Slowly add the milk, stirring until thick and smooth. Add pepper.

Remove from heat, and add to cheese mixture. Beat well.

Place a layer of *phyllo* pastry sheets in an 11 by 14 by 2-inch lightly buttered pan. Brush with melted butter. Cover with 5 more layers of pastry sheets, brushing each sheet with melted butter before adding another. Fill with cheese mixture and then place 8 layers of pastry sheets over filling, again brushing each layer with melted butter. Keep *phyllo* pastry sheets covered with a slightly damp cloth while you are working with them, as they tend to dry out very quickly.

Place in a preheated 350° oven, and bake 30 minutes or until surface is lightly browned.

Cut into small squares. Spear each square with a cocktail pick to hold filling and pastry together. Serve warm.

Serves 6 to 8.

ROQUEFORT-CHEESE PUFFS

¼ pound Roquefort cheese
1 pint cottage cheese
2 eggs, lightly beaten
Sprinkling of salt

½ pound Greek *phyllo* pastry sheets
¼ pound butter, melted and slightly cooled

Crumble Roquefort cheese. Add cottage cheese, and blend. Add eggs and salt, and mix well.

Cut off a portion of a sheet of the *phyllo* pastry about 6 inches long and 4 inches wide, and brush it with melted butter. Place about 1 tablespoon of the cheese mixture toward one end of the pastry. Fold up once, then turn in the sides, and roll up. Brush with butter on all sides, and place on a long baking sheet. Repeat until all pastry and filling have been used. Keep unused pastry sheets covered with a damp cloth to prevent drying out. (*Pastry may be made ahead to this point. Keep covered with a damp cloth until time to bake. Brush with melted butter just before baking.*)

Bake in a preheated 425° oven until lightly browned.

Serve warm.

Serves 6 to 8.

2

Stock—Beautiful Stock!

Does homemade, slowly cooked stock belong in a quick-cooking cookbook when canned consommé and soup are such easy substitutes?

It certainly does. There is simply no other way to achieve superb flavor, especially in quick-cooking meals. Everything you prepare in minutes with stock tastes as if you had spent hours in the kitchen. In fact, once you have tried cooking with stock, nothing will induce you to go back to chemical-laden and tinny-tasting commercial substitutes.

Stock only *sounds* complicated and time-consuming. It is really as easy as boiling water; any novice cook can do it. Although it has to be simmered for hours, you do not have to remain in a hot kitchen to simmer along with it. In fact, you can leave. Play golf, go shopping, or simply plug away at other chores; stock will do nicely without you. You can even let it cook overnight if that's more convenient for you.

Preparing the ingredients for a stockpot requires no more than 10 to 15 minutes. Straining stock once it has been cooked and storing it in your refrigerator takes no more than another 10 to 15 minutes, and this includes washing up. Sufficient stock can be made to last a week or a month, and as long as you have it on hand, your daily cooking chores will be so greatly lessened you'll wonder how you ever managed without it. As Escoffier said, "If one's stock is good, what remains of the cooking is easy."

Any chef worth his salt knows this. I will never forget a visit to the kitchens of Air France: Huge stockpots were in place on the back of the

21

stoves, and every scrap of meat and vegetables left over from cooking was scrupulously added to the constantly simmering pots. The result: airline food that is undoubtedly the best in the skies.

The long slow cooking required releases the natural gelatin from the bones, which is almost pure protein. This thickening quality and deep-down flavor make heavenly sauces, soups, casseroles, and so on. It is, in fact, the secret of quick-cooking French soups and sauces. This clear fat-free base is unexcelled in delicate subtle flavor. It is also a fact that the low-fat, high-protein content of stock can produce strong nails, healthy hair, and a svelte figure. Could you ask for more?

This chapter consists of just two recipes, one for beef stock and one for chicken, but there is a bonus in each one: a way to cook a main dish while you are at it.

BEEF STOCK

2 pounds shank of beef with bone in
1 pound beef marrow bones
1 large onion, peeled and quartered
2 medium carrots, scraped and cut into quarters
2 cups dry red wine
1 3-pound brisket of beef
½ cup chopped celery tops
¼ cup chopped parsley
2 teaspoons salt
6 to 8 peppercorns
1 bay leaf

Put beef shank, marrow bones, onion, and carrot in a large roasting pan. Place in a preheated 450° oven for 30 to 45 minutes or until bones and meat are browned. Turn them occasionally so that they brown evenly on all sides.

Remove pan from oven, and transfer meat, bones, and vegetables to a large (8-to-10-quart) soup pot. Pour 1 cup of the wine into the roasting pan, and scrape all the brown bits and pieces of meat and vegetables that have clung to the pan into it. Add this to the soup pot, then add the second cup of the wine, the remaining ingredients, and sufficient water to come to about 2 inches of rim of pot.

Bring to a full boil. Turn heat to very low, partially cover pot with a loosely fitting lid, and let simmer for about 2 hours.

Remove brisket of beef to a large platter. Cool, then cover and refrigerate.

Add additional water to pot to again come to 2 inches of rim, and continue to cook stock over low heat for at least 4 hours, or let simmer very slowly overnight.

Turn off heat, and cool.

When cool, strain into containers, and refrigerate 6 hours or overnight. Remove from refrigerator, and discard all fat that has congealed on the surface.

Cover stock, and return to refrigerator. Use within 1 week, or cover, seal, and store in freezer, and use within 6 weeks.

Your bonus? Sufficient brisket of beef to serve 4 to 6. Serve cold with horseradish sauce and potato salad, or reheat in stock and serve hot with new potatoes and carrots cooked in the same stock.

CHICKEN STOCK

1 3½-to-4-pound whole chicken
2 pounds chicken necks and wings
1 large white onion, peeled and quartered
1 large carrot, scraped and cut into thick slices
½ cup celery tops

¼ cup chopped parsley
1 bay leaf
4 to 6 allspice berries
2 teaspoons salt
¼ teaspoon freshly ground black pepper
1 cup dry white wine

Place whole chicken and chicken necks and wings in a large (8-to-10-quart) soup pot. Add water to cover, and bring to a boil. Lower heat, and skim surface until clear. Add remaining ingredients plus sufficient water to come to about 2 inches of rim of pot. Cover partially with a loose-fitting lid. Let simmer until whole chicken is tender, about 1½ hours.

Remove whole chicken, and let cool sufficiently to handle. Remove skin and bones from meat. Dice meat, place in a covered bowl, and refrigerate. Discard skin. Return bones to stockpot.

Continue to cook stock with bones for 2½ to 3 hours, or add sufficient water to come to rim of pot, and let simmer very slowly overnight.

When cool, strain into containers, and refrigerate 6 hours or overnight. Then remove from refrigerator, and discard all the fat congealed on the surface.

Cover and return stock to refrigerator to use within 1 week, or cover, seal, and freeze, and use within 6 weeks.

Your bonus? Sufficient cold diced boiled chicken to make 4 to 6 servings of chicken à la king, chicken hash, salad, or what (recipe) have you.

3

Absolutely-Delicious-Anytime Soups
(Made in 15 to 30 Minutes)

Soup? Who makes soup? Canned, frozen, and dehydrated soups, all ready to heat and eat, are right there on your supermarket shelves in unlimited variety. Well, commercially prepared soups may keep you from starving, but they can't and won't give you the honest down-right pleasure and enjoyment—or the nutrition—of real soup.

Many Americans avoid homemade soup because they are only familiar with the "peasant-style" variety. And it is true that such soups are often overheavy and greasy. Moreover they take a lot of work and time to prepare. This is by no means the whole homemade-soup story, as the French well know. In that country elegant and sophisticated soups are prepared quickly from a base of clear fat-free stock.

There are few more delightful lunches than hot and creamy townhouse mushroom soup; a salad of avocado, tomatoes, and chives; and a (made-ahead) ice-cream pie. Or on a hot day you can't beat a cold, delicate watercress soup, chicken sandwiches, and a frosty bowl of fresh fruit.

Soup can be the beginning or the middle of a nutritious but quickly cooked meal. It can be a midnight supper or Sunday lunch. It can be the answer to easy entertaining or an entire family meal, but to be at its delicious best, it must be homemade.

If you can spare 15 to 30 minutes, you can prepare a great soup, a soup with character—completely unlike the canned varieties, or for that matter the heavy, greasy old-fashioned soups that Grandmother did indeed take hours to make.

Tips on Cooking and Serving Soups

Garnish cream soups with salted whipped cream or sour cream. Creamed soups also welcome minced chives or watercress.

A little crumbled crisp-cooked bacon enhances some creamed soups, as do toasted almond slivers or chopped pistachio nuts.

Vegetable soups—all kinds—are improved if just before serving you add a little of the vegetable used in the soup, freshly chopped; for example, freshly chopped mushrooms to mushroom soup, chopped celery to celery soup, chopped tomato to cream of tomato soup, etc.

Just a suggestion of curry powder does great things to many soups, and a jigger of dry sherry goes well in almost all soups.

Try floating thin slices of avocado, lightly marinated in lemon juice, on black bean soup, cream of mushroom and celery soups, or thick creamy tomato soup.

TOWN-HOUSE MUSHROOM SOUP

½ pound fresh mushrooms	3 or 4 dashes Tabasco sauce
3 cups Chicken or Beef Stock (pages 22–24)	¼ cup dry sherry Salt
1 tablespoon butter	White pepper
2 teaspoons flour	Whipped cream
1 cup milk	Curry powder

Place mushrooms and stock in a saucepan, and let simmer over low heat for 10 minutes. Cool slightly, then pour into electric blender, and blend until very smooth.

Melt the butter in a second large saucepan, and stir in the flour. When smooth, slowly add the mushroom stock, stirring as it is added. Cook, stirring, over low heat until mixture thickens slightly. Add the milk, Tabasco, and sherry, and continue to cook and stir until steamy hot. Season to taste with salt and pepper.

Ladle into deep soup bowls. Place a teaspoon of unsweetened whipped cream on each, and sprinkle, but lightly, with curry powder.

Serves 4 to 6.

CHICKEN ALMOND SOUP WITH AVOCADO

½ cup blanched almonds
½ cup diced cooked chicken
1 cup light cream
3 cups Chicken Stock (pages 23–24)

Salt
White pepper
1 medium avocado
Lemon juice

Place almonds, chicken, cream, and ½ cup stock in electric blender, and blend until smooth.

Pour mixture into the top half of a double boiler. Add remaining chicken stock, and season lightly with salt and pepper. Place over hot water, and let steam for 10 to 15 minutes.

Peel and halve avocado, discarding pit. Cut into thin slices, and sprinkle with lemon juice.

Place soup over direct heat until very hot. Do not allow to boil.

Put 2 or 3 slices of avocado in each serving bowl, and ladle the hot soup over them.

Serves 4 to 6.

SOUPE À LA NAPOLEON

¼ cup butter
½ pound small white onions, peeled and finely chopped
1 cup dry white wine
3 cups Chicken Stock (pages 23–24)

½ pound Port du Salut cheese, crumbled
Salt
White pepper
1 cup croutons
1 tablespoon butter
2 tablespoons minced parsley

Place the ¼ cup butter and the onions in a saucepan over low heat, and cook, stirring, until onions are limp but not browned. Transfer to a blender, and blend until smooth (or force through a sieve).

Combine onion mixture with wine and stock. Cook, stirring, until steamy hot (do not allow to boil). Add cheese, and continue to cook and stir until cheese has melted. Season with salt and pepper.

Place croutons in a large soup tureen, and pour the hot soup over them. Dot with slivers of the 1 tablespoon butter, and sprinkle with parsley.

Ladle into bowls, and pass additional croutons if desired.

Serves 6.

CREAM OF CHICKEN SOUP

5 cups Chicken Stock (pages 23–24)	Curry powder
	1 egg yolk, lightly beaten
Salt	½ cup heavy cream
Pepper	½ cup diced cooked chicken
Garlic salt	¼ cup grated Swiss cheese

Place stock in saucepan, and bring to boil. Lower heat, and season lightly with salt, pepper, garlic salt, and curry powder. Let simmer 8 to 10 minutes.

Mix egg yolk with cream, and add 2 to 3 tablespoons of the simmering stock, stirring quickly to blend. Add mixture to stock, and stir until blended. Add diced chicken, and cook a final 5 minutes. Do not allow to boil.

Add Swiss cheese, and serve very hot with buttered and toasted crackers.

It's the Swiss cheese that adds that special something.

Serves 6.

PUREE OF MARRON SOUP

2 tablespoons butter	1 cup milk
1 tablespoon flour	¼ cup dry sherry
3 cups Chicken or Beef Stock (pages 22–24)	Salt
	Pepper
½ cup unsweetened marron puree	2 tablespoons chopped chives

Melt the butter in a large saucepan over low heat. Stir in the flour, and blend well. Slowly add the stock, stirring as it is added.

Add marron puree, and continue to stir until mixture is smooth. Let simmer 5 to 10 minutes, stirring frequently.

Pour in the milk and sherry, and cook, stirring, until soup is steamy hot. Season to taste with salt and pepper. Add chives, and serve.

Serves 4 to 6.

SHRIMP BISQUE

2 slices white bread
2 tablespoons butter
1 pound cooked shrimp, shelled, deveined, and coarsely chopped
2 tablespoons minced green onion
2 tablespoons minced parsley
¼ teaspoon pepper

1 cup tomato juice
2 cups Chicken Stock (pages 23– 24)
1 bay leaf
1 cup light cream
½ teaspoon salt

Sprinkle bread slices with sufficient water to soften. Then mash with a fork.

Melt the butter in a saucepan. Add the shrimp, onion, parsley, and bread. Cook, stirring, over low heat, 2 to 3 minutes. Season with salt and pepper.

Pour in the tomato juice and chicken stock. Stir to blend. Add the bay leaf, and let steam over low heat 5 to 10 minutes. Do not allow to boil. Add the cream, and continue to cook only until steamy hot. Remove bay leaf.

Serves 4 to 6.

CLAM CONSOMMÉ

2 cups Chicken Stock (pages 23– 24)
1 cup tomato juice
1 cup clam broth
1 slice of onion

1 sprig of parsley
1 slice of lemon
Salt
White pepper

Combine stock, tomato juice, and clam broth in saucepan. Add onion, parsley, and lemon. Place over low heat, and let barely simmer for 10 minutes. Discard onion, parsley, and lemon. Season to taste with salt and pepper. Serve steamy hot.

Serves 4 to 6.

COLD WATERCRESS SOUP

¾ cup chopped watercress
3 cups Chicken Stock (pages 23–24)
½ teaspoon sugar
1 egg yolk

2 cups light cream
Salt
Pepper
Sour cream

Place ½ cup of the chopped watercress, 1 cup of stock, and the sugar in a saucepan, and let it simmer over low heat for 10 minutes. Strain through a fine sieve into a second saucepan, and add remaining stock.

Beat egg yolk with cream until blended, and add to stock mixture.

Stir over low heat until soup thickens slightly. Do not allow to boil. Season with salt and pepper to taste.

Remove from heat, and cool. Refrigerate until well chilled. Garnish each portion with a little sour cream, and sprinkle with remaining chopped watercress.

Serves 6.

LES HALLES ONION SOUP

French onion soup is a soup to serve for a midnight soup supper. This version calls for real crusty French bread, buttered and heated but not toasted dry. Serve this, then a rich cake-and-ice-cream-and-sauce dessert and freshly made coffee. It's a combination your guests will rave about long after.

1 pound purple (Italian) onions
4 tablespoons butter
6 cups Chicken or Beef Stock (pages 22–24)

6 small slices French bread
1 8-ounce package French Bonée or Port du Salut cheese, well chilled

Peel the onions, and cut into paper-thin slices.

Melt the butter in a large saucepan. Add the onion slices, and cook them over medium heat until they are lightly browned. Stir and turn them constantly to prevent burning.

Turn heat very low, add the stock, and let simmer 10 to 15 minutes. Remove from heat, and let stand 1 hour or longer.

When time to serve, toast the French bread. Cut the cheese cross-wise into six round slices, using a sharp warm knife.

Reheat the soup, and pour it into 6 individual earthenware oven-proof casseroles. Float 1 slice of toast in each casserole, and cover with 1 slice of cheese. Place under a medium broiler flame until the cheese is melted and bubbly hot. Serve at once.

Serves 6.

FRESH TOMATO SOUP

2 large ripe tomatoes, chopped	1 bay leaf
1 medium onion, peeled and chopped	Salt
	Pepper
1 tablespoon butter	Oregano
3 cups Chicken Stock (pages 23–24)	1 cup light cream
	Chopped parsley

In a saucepan sauté the tomatoes and onion in the butter until the onion is limp. Add the stock and bay leaf. Season lightly with salt and pepper, and add a sprinkling of oregano. Let simmer over low heat 15 to 20 minutes. Remove bay leaf.

Strain soup through a colander that has been lined with cheese-cloth (or through a very fine sieve) into a second pot. Place over low heat, add the cream, and cook, stirring occasionally, until steamy hot. Correct seasoning with additional salt and pepper as needed. Sprinkle each serving with chopped parsley just before serving.

Serves 4 to 6.

4

Salad Dressings and Salad-Making Made Easy

Salad Dressings

What's a salad without the dressing? And what's a *superb* salad without homemade dressing? A lot of trouble? Nothing could be less. It takes only minutes, and it saves dollars and dollars—but more important it saves your salad ingredients from the chemicals and flavor preservatives that would spoil their taste.

As to time, French dressing takes no more than 5 minutes to prepare and mayonnaise no more than a few. No special skill is required, and there are endless variations on these two classic themes.

BASIC FRENCH DRESSING

¼ cup vinegar (cider, red wine, white wine, tarragon or any other herb-flavored vinegar) or fresh lemon juice or half fresh lemon juice and half fresh orange juice

1 teaspoon salt or to taste

¼ teaspoon freshly ground pepper or to taste

Herbs, as desired

Other seasoning, as desired

¾ cup oil (olive oil, peanut oil, or any other preferred oil)

Combine vinegar, salt, pepper, herbs, and any other desired seasoning. If dry herbs are used, let mixture stand at room temperature for 45

33

minutes to 1 hour. Add oil, and beat vigorously with a fork or a rotary beater.

Make ahead if desired, but beat vigorously again, just before using.

Makes about 1 cup dressing.

Before adding oil you may add to the vinegar any of the following:

½ to 1 teaspoon sugar (Try this on people who claim they don't like French dressing.)

¾ to 1 teaspoon paprika

½ to 1 teaspoon curry powder

Few drops Tabasco sauce and/or Worcestershire sauce

½ to 1 teaspoon dried basil or tarragon or a pinch of oregano

1 to 2 teaspoons chopped fresh tarragon, basil, or mint

1 to 2 teaspoons chopped chives, shallots, or scallions

1 small clove garlic, minced

2 to 3 tablespoons well-drained freshly ground horseradish and/or 2 to 3 tablespoons chopped fresh apples or pears

½ cup (bottled) chili sauce

1 tablespoon celery seed or sesame seed

1 large fresh tomato, peeled, seeded, and finely chopped

2 to 4 chopped anchovy fillets

2 to 4 chopped pitted black olives

Or add to prepared dressing:

⅓ to ½ cup sour cream (mixed well) and/or 2 to 3 teaspoons finely chopped capers or chopped radishes

1 to 2 tablespoons Major Gray chutney, larger pieces finely chopped

BASIC MAYONNAISE

2 egg yolks

1 tablespoon lemon juice

½ teaspoon salt

¼ teaspoon pepper

¼ to ½ teaspoon dry mustard

1¼ cups oil

1 tablespoon vinegar (white wine, cider, or tarragon)

Blender Method

Place egg yolks, lemon juice, salt, pepper, mustard, and ¼ cup of the oil in container of electric blender. Blend at high speed for 10 seconds. Reduce speed to low. Remove cover, and add half of the remaining oil in a slow steady stream. Add vinegar, turn speed to high, and add remaining oil, again in a slow steady stream.

Makes about 2 cups. Refrigerate until ready to use.

To Make without a Blender

Place egg yolks in a deep mixing bowl, and beat with a wire whisk until thick and lemon-colored. Add lemon juice, salt, pepper, and mustard. Beat well. Now slowly start to add the oil, at first drop by drop, then in a slow steady stream, beating constantly as it is added. Continue beating until mixture thickens. Add vinegar, and beat a final half minute. *Note:* If you place crumpled paper toweling or a folded dishcloth under the bowl to put it at a slight angle, the bowl will stay put while you simultaneously beat the mixture and add the oil.

Makes about 2 cups.

Some things you can add to prepared mayonnaise singly or in combinations of three or four:

2 to 4 tablespoons chopped parsley, watercress, pimiento, anchovy fillets, or sweet mixed pickles

2 to 3 tablespoons finely diced green pepper, celery, chives, fresh tarragon, or fresh basil

About ¼ cup crumbled Roquefort cheese, blue cheese, or feta cheese

1 teaspoon grated orange rind or lemon rind

2 to 4 tablespoons chopped water chestnuts, almonds, pecans, or candied ginger

1 to 2 tablespoons finely chopped pistachio nuts

You may also fold into 1¾ cups prepared mayonnaise:

½ to ¾ cup sour cream

½ to ¾ cup salted whipped cream

¼ to ½ cup (bottled) chili sauce

2 to 3 tablespoons tomato catsup

1 to 2 tablespoons tomato puree

GREEN MAYONNAISE

5 or 6 leaves raw spinach, finely   3 or 4 scallions, finely chopped
   chopped   Basic Mayonnaise (pages 34–35)

Add spinach and scallions to the ¼ cup oil in the first step of the Basic Mayonnaise recipe. Blend until smooth in electric blender. Proceed as in making Basic Mayonnaise.

Makes about 2 cups.

LOUISIANA MUSTARD MAYONNAISE

3 hard-cooked eggs   ¼ teaspoon freshly ground black
1 egg yolk   pepper
2 tablespoons tarragon vinegar   ½ teaspoon sugar
2 teaspoons prepared mustard   1 cup oil
¼ teaspoon salt or more to taste

Separate egg yolks from egg whites. In a small bowl mash yolks with a fork until smooth. Place whites on a chopping board, and chop fine.

Combine egg yolk, vinegar, mustard, salt, pepper, and sugar in a large mixing bowl, and beat with a wire whisk until well blended.

Add mashed hard-cooked egg yolks alternately with the oil, beating well after each addition. Continue to beat until mixture is thick and smooth.

Fold in chopped egg whites, or reserve them to use as a garnish.

Makes about 1¾ cups mayonnaise.

BACON DRESSING

4 slices bacon   ½ teaspoon freshly ground black
1 teaspoon sugar   pepper
      ⅓ cup vinegar

Cook bacon in a heavy skillet over low heat until fat has rendered and bacon is crisp. Remove bacon to paper toweling. Drain and crumble.

To the hot rendered fat in the skillet add the sugar, pepper, vinegar, and crumbled bacon. Mix well, and pour over salad while still warm.

This is a great dressing for raw spinach or any salad of mixed greens. Also great for potato salad.

Makes about ¾ cup dressing.

SAUCE VINAIGRETTE WITH MINCED VEGETABLES

2 or 3 green onions
¼ green pepper, seeded
2 or 3 sprigs parsley
1 canned pimiento
¼ cup mixed sweet pickles, well drained
1 cup salad oil
⅓ cup white-wine vinegar
1 teaspoon sugar
1 teaspoon salt
½ teaspoon freshly ground black pepper
1 small clove garlic, peeled

Mince very fine the onion, pepper, parsley, pimiento, and pickles.

Place in a bowl or jar with the remaining ingredients. Cover and refrigerate several hours before using. Remove garlic before serving.

Makes about 2 cups sauce.

AVOCADO AND ORANGE-JUICE DRESSING

1 large very ripe avocado
2 tablespoons corn or peanut oil
½ cup fresh orange juice
½ teaspoon salt
¼ teaspoon freshly ground black pepper

Peel the avocado, and remove the seed. Place in a mixing bowl, and mash until very smooth. Add remaining ingredients, and whip with a fork or wire whisk until blended and frothy. Pour over prepared greens, toss well, and serve.

Makes about ½ cup dressing.

Salads

What's new and what's news about salads in the seventies? To begin with, salads have gained in importance. Served as a first course, as an important part of the buffet table, or as a hearty accompaniment to a light main course, they have become more substantial fare.

The California idea of starting the meal with a salad of crisp greens, vegetables, and fruit, then serving just one hot dish, is more popular than ever. Light and low-calorie main-course salads have replaced the calorie-laden creamed dishes once so popular at so-called ladies' luncheons. And an assortment of interesting and hearty salads is often all that is served for an informal "help-yourself" party meal.

More work for the cook? No, of course not; there is far less. A first-course salad can replace the hot vegetable otherwise served with the main course. Main-course salads mean less cooking and less time in the kitchen, and salads for parties can be made ahead.

Included in this chapter are "light-overture" salads, "main-act" salads, and salads that play an important supporting part in the meal.

First-Course Salads

Here are combinations that have that extra touch. All salads serve 4 to 6. Before you begin:

Wash all greens well. Place in a salad basket, and shake off water. Turn out onto paper toweling, and gently but thoroughly blot away every last trace of moisture. Remove and discard tough stems and bruised leaves.

Peel and slice or dice other vegetables and fruits.

Always sprinkle peeled, seeded, and sliced or diced avocado and such fresh fruits as apples or pears with lemon juice to prevent discoloration.

Combine:

1 pound very crisp and fresh spinach, 1 cup ripe but still firm chunks of avocado, ½ cup thinly sliced strawberries, and 2 tablespoons finely minced chives.

Toss with ¼ to ½ cup garlicky French dressing.

Combine:

2 medium heads Boston lettuce, torn into bite-size pieces; 1 medium purple onion, peeled and cut into paper-thin slices, each slice broken into rings; 1 large navel orange, peeled, seeded, and chopped; and 6 large fresh mushrooms, trimmed and thinly sliced.

Toss with ¼ to ½ cup French dressing. Garnish with small balls of cream cheese mixed with a little sour cream and rolled in finely ground pecans.

Combine:

2 heads of Bibb lettuce, torn into bite-size pieces; 1 small bunch watercress, separated into small sprigs; 6 to 12 small ripe melon balls; 4 ounces crumbled blue or Roquefort cheese; and 1 2-ounce can anchovy fillets, chopped.

Toss with ¼ to ½ cup French dressing. Just before serving add ½ cup crisp garlicky croutons.

Combine:

2 Belgian endives, trimmed and cut into bite-size pieces; 1 avocado, peeled, seeded, and chopped; 1 cup diced fresh pineapple; ½ cup diced fresh strawberries, cut in half; 1 banana, peeled and sliced; and 2 tablespoons finely minced chives.

Dress with Basic Mayonnaise (pages 34–35). Serve on large lettuce leaves. Garnish with springs of watercress.

Combine:

½ pound fresh spinach, chopped; 1 small bunch watercress, chopped; 2 stalks celery, chopped; 1 pound boiled shrimp, shelled, de-veined, and chopped; ¼ cup (bottled) chili sauce; and ¼ cup Basic

Mayonnaise (pages 34–35) that has first been mixed with ¼ teaspoon Tabasco sauce and 1 tablespoon horseradish.

Toss well, and chill.

Perfect-for-a-Picnic Salad

When a substantial salad is needed, here is an old standby but with a real flavor difference.

POTATO SALAD WITH SOUR-CREAM DRESSING

3 cups diced boiled potatoes
1 cup diced peeled apple
½ cup finely chopped celery
¼ cup minced onion
1 small can sardines, drained and chopped
½ cup sour cream

¼ cup mayonnaise
1 tablespoon vinegar
Salt
Pepper
Lettuce
2 hard-cooked eggs, sliced
Sweet mixed pickles

Place potatoes, apple, celery, onion, and sardines in salad bowl.

Combine sour cream, mayonnaise, vinegar, and salt and pepper. Pour over potato mixture.

Mix gently but well.

Cover and refrigerate for 1 hour or longer.

Serve on lettuce leaves. Garnish with sliced hard-cooked eggs and sweet mixed pickles.

Serves 6 to 8.

Salad for a Buffet Table

WALDORF COLESLAW

1 small head cabbage
2 large crisp apples
1 small white onion
6 stalks celery
1 8-ounce can crushed pineapple, thoroughly drained

Salt
Pepper
Paprika
Basic Mayonnaise (pages 34–35)

Remove outer leaves from cabbage, and chop very fine.

Peel and core apples. Peel onion. Chop apples, onion, and celery very fine.

Place chopped ingredients in salad bowl. Add well-drained pineapple.

Season to taste with salt, pepper, and paprika.

Mix with sufficient mayonnaise to moisten generously.

This salad is best if flavors are allowed to blend and mellow. Cover with plastic wrap or foil, and refrigerate 2 hours or longer before serving.
Serves 8 to 10.

Luncheon Salad

Here is a salad created for a diet menu but so good it's served at our house at least once a week. It is excellent with a cold-meat platter luncheon.

CHOPPED VEGETABLE SALAD

3 to 4 medium carrots, scraped
1 medium turnip, peeled
4 to 6 stalks celery
2 large crisp apples, peeled and cored
1 small white onion, peeled
½ cup seedless raisins
½ cup chopped almonds or canned water chestnuts (optional)
3 parts oil and 1 part vinegar, or Basic Mayonnaise (pages 34–35)
Salt
Pepper

Grate the carrots and turnip on the medium-fine side of your grater. Chop celery, apples, and onion very fine.

Combine vegetables. Add raisins and, if desired, almonds or water chestnuts. Mix well.

Dress with oil and vinegar, using only enough to moisten mixture, or dress with homemade mayonnaise, again using only enough to moisten. Season with salt and pepper.
Serves 4.

International Vegetable Salad

This selection for a large buffet party consists of Salade de Safran Riz, Swedish Cucumber Salad, Mexican Corn Salad, and Aubergine à la Turque. To be served on your largest platter, each component part should be arranged separately one after the other to form an attractive design.

Prepare all salads ahead, and chill well. Arrange on platter just before serving.

Garnish the platter with black and green olives and watercress. All that is needed to complete the meal is a beverage and an attractive basket filled with an assortment of hot buttered rolls. The beverage may be beer, a good white wine, or if it's to be a really festive party, champagne.

SALADE DE SAFRAN RIZ
(Saffron Rice Salad)

½ teaspoon saffron threads
½ cup warm water
1 10-ounce package frozen green peas
2½ cups water
1¼ cups Italian imported rice or long-grained converted white rice
1 clove garlic, peeled
1 teaspoon oil
½ teaspoon salt
½ cup ripe-olive slivers
½ cup pimiento
½ cup chopped celery
2 tablespoons finely minced scallions
2 tablespoons finely minced parsley
6 or 8 canned water chestnuts
¼ cup French dressing or more if desired
Black olives
Pimiento-stuffed green olives
Parsley sprigs
Radishes

Soak the saffron threads in the warm water for 30 minutes. Strain water, and discard saffron.

Remove frozen green peas from package, and let thaw at room temperature for 30 minutes.

Bring the 2½ cups of water and the ½ cup saffron water to a full boil in a large saucepan. Slowly add the rice a few grains at a time so that water continues to boil. Add garlic, oil, and salt. Reduce heat, and let simmer for 20 to 25 minutes or until rice is tender and almost all water has evaporated. There should be about 1 tablespoon water in the bottom of the pan. Remove from heat, and discard garlic.

Add the thawed green peas, and gently stir them into the rice with a fork. Cover pan, and continue to cook for 1 minute. Then remove from heat, and let stand covered for 8 to 10 minutes or until rice is completely dry and peas are tender.

Transfer rice and peas to a large salad bowl, and refrigerate until well chilled. Add remaining ingredients except for the last 4, and toss lightly to blend. Chill 1 hour or longer before serving.

Garnish with olives, parsley, and radishes.

Serves 6 to 8.

SWEDISH CUCUMBER SALAD

6 medium cucumbers	¾ teaspoon freshly ground black
1 cup sour cream	pepper
1 teaspoon salt	1 tablespoon grated horseradish

Peel cucumbers. Score lengthwise with fork tines. Cut into paper-thin slices.

Combine sour cream, salt, pepper, and horseradish. Blend and pour over cucumbers. Toss lightly. Chill until ready to serve.

Serves 6 to 8.

MEXICAN CORN SALAD

3 cups cooked corn kernels (best if fresh from the cob but frozen or canned can substitute)
1 small green pepper, seeded and diced
1 small white onion, peeled and diced
2 stalks celery, diced

1 large tomato, seeded and diced
1 teaspoon salt
½ teaspoon freshly ground black pepper
3 tablespoons Basic Mayonnaise (pages 34–35)
1 tablespoon lemon juice

Combine vegetables, and sprinkle with salt and pepper. Add mayonnaise and lemon juice. Toss and chill.

Serves 6 to 8.

AUBERGINE À LA TURQUE
(Eggplant Salad Mediterranean Style)

1 medium eggplant, peeled and chopped
Flour
¾ cup olive oil or more if needed
1 large purple onion, peeled and chopped
1 medium green pepper, seeded and chopped

4 large tomatoes, peeled, seeded, and chopped
Salt
Freshly ground black pepper
1 clove garlic, finely minced
1 teaspoon sugar
1 tablespoon tarragon vinegar

Dredge eggplant lightly with flour. Heat the oil in a heavy skillet, add the eggplant, and sauté over medium heat until lightly browned, 8 to 10 minutes. Add additional oil if needed. Add remaining vegetables. Season with salt and pepper. Add minced garlic. Lower heat, and let simmer until mixture thickens, about 45 minutes. Stir occasionally.

Remove from heat, and stir in sugar and vinegar. Correct seasoning with additional salt and pepper as needed. Cool slightly, then refrigerate, covered, until about ½ hour before serving.

Serve cool but not overchilled.

Very thin slices of French or dark rye bread are the perfect accompaniment.

Serves 6 to 8.

Main-Course Salad

BOUILLABAISSE SALAD

1 pound lump crabmeat
¼ cup Basic French Dressing (pages 33–34)
2 tablespoons capers
2 pounds new potatoes, cooked and peeled
3 tablespoons tarragon vinegar
2 tablespoons salad oil
1 teaspoon salt
¼ teaspoon freshly ground black pepper
2 tablespoons minced chives
1 head romaine lettuce
2 tablespoons olive oil
1 tablespoon white-wine vinegar
½ teaspoon salt
¼ teaspoon pepper
¼ teaspoon dry mustard
1 clove garlic, minced
2 tablespoons grated Parmesan cheese
2 small cold boiled lobsters, each split in half
8 large cold boiled shrimp
4 large oysters on the half shell
1 tablespoon lemon juice
2 tablespoons caviar
Black olives
Tomato wedges
Wedges of hard-cooked egg
Basic Mayonnaise (pages 34–35)
Chili sauce (bottled)

Combine crabmeat, French dressing, and capers, and chill.

Dice potatoes while still warm. Combine tarragon vinegar, salad oil, salt, pepper, and chives. Blend well, and pour over diced potatoes. Chill.

Tear lettuce into medium-size pieces. Combine olive oil, wine vinegar, salt, pepper, mustard, garlic, and cheese. Beat with a fork or a rotary beater until thoroughly blended. Pour over lettuce, and toss well.

Arrange prepared lettuce salad on 4 dinner plates. Place one half lobster in the center of each. Add to each plate 2 shrimp, 1 oyster on shell, a mound of the chilled crabmeat, and a serving of the cold potatoes. Sprinkle oyster with lemon juice and caviar. Garnish each plate with black olives, tomato wedges, and wedges of hard-cooked egg.

Combine equal parts mayonnaise and chili sauce. Pour into a sauceboat, and pass at the table.

Serves 4.

5

Quick-to-the-Table Luncheon, Supper, and Dinner Dishes

After a hard day's work or for that matter a hard day's play who wants to spend time in the kitchen? Not me, and I think not you. But that's still no reason to turn to nutrition-low, high-cost, and tasteless commercially prepared TV dinners when delicious meals, nourishing meals, and even elegant meals can be prepared in short order—not an old-fashioned turkey dinner with all the trimmings but something just as good and often better.

Here is a collection of main-course dishes that can be prepared in 10 to 30 minutes with a minimum of work. Start with a first-course salad, and take a made-ahead dessert from the freezer. For many, quick-cooking rice or noodles complete the meal; for others good crusty French- or Italian-style bread is all that is needed.

Brew some coffee, make iced tea, or open a bottle of good wine, and lunch or supper is ready to serve.

Quickies

SHRIMP SCAMPI

Split 12 raw jumbo shrimp up the back with a sharp knife or with kitchen shears. Remove shell, and devein. Split down the insides, being careful not to cut through the shrimp. Spread open like butterflies.

47

Heat ¼ cup olive oil in a heavy skillet. Add shrimp, and sauté 3 minutes over medium heat. Now add ½ stick (¼ cup) butter cut into bits, a peeled and minced clove of garlic, ¼ cup minced parsley, and 1 tablespoon lemon juice. Sprinkle with salt, and cook, stirring often, for a final 4 minutes.

Serve with crusty Italian bread to mop up the sauce.

Serves 2.

Takes about 14 minutes to prepare and cook. It's to be served after the antipasto and pasta, before the fresh fruit and cheese.

QUICK BIFTECK À LA RUSSE

Make 4 patties from 1 pound of twice-ground top round of beef. Season with salt, pepper, and garlic salt. Dredge with flour.

Melt 2 tablespoons butter with 1 tablespoon oil in a heavy skillet. Add meat patties, and cook over medium heat 2 minutes on each side. Remove to warm plates.

Add 2 tablespoons finely minced onion to the skillet, and stir a half minute. Reduce heat slightly, and pour in ½ cup sour cream. Season with salt, pepper, and paprika. Heat thoroughly, but do not allow to boil. Pour over meat patties, and serve.

Serves 2 or 4, depending on how hungry.

Takes about 10 minutes to prepare and cook. Suggested go-with: steamed new potatoes, well buttered and parslied. Cold borscht might be your beginning; fresh strawberries sprinkled with sugar and kirsch your dessert.

WIENER SCHNITZEL

Buy 1 pound veal cut from the leg. Have it cut into 4 slices and pounded thin.

Beat 2 eggs in a shallow bowl with 1 tablespoon water until blended.

Spread out 1 cup fine dry bread crumbs on waxed paper. Mix in ¼ teaspoon each salt, pepper, and paprika.

Dip each veal slice first in egg, then in crumbs. Press crumbs into meat.

Heat 1 tablespoon butter with 1 tablespoon oil in a large skillet. Add 2 slices of the veal, and cook them over medium heat until golden on both sides, about 2 minutes. Remove to a warm platter. Add a second tablespoon each butter and oil to the skillet, and repeat with remaining meat.

Sprinkle each piece with chopped parsley, and serve with wedges of lemon.

Serves 4.

Takes about 12 minutes to prepare and cook. It goes well with buttered flat noodles. Serve a salad of sliced nicely ripened tomatoes and paper-thin slices of cucumber, and you'll end up with something special in flavor and only two pans to wash.

CHIPPED BEEF IN SOUR CREAM

Take a large-size can of dried chipped beef. Remove contents, and tear into shreds. Sauté in 2 tablespoons butter until nicely heated. Pour in ¾ cup sour cream. Season with pepper—no salt needed—and add ½ cup chopped (canned) water chestnuts. Let heat but not boil. Serve over toast.

Serves 2.

An old English standby updated, this takes only about 6 minutes to prepare and cook. Try baked tomato halves as an accompaniment.

DEVILED OYSTERS AND SHRIMP

Sauté ¼ cup chopped onion in 2 tablespoons butter for a half minute in a large heavy skillet. Add 1½ cups of preferably homemade tomato sauce, 1 teaspoon Worcestershire sauce, a dash of Tabasco sauce, and a teaspoon prepared mustard. Cook, stirring now and again, until heated. Add 1 pint drained oysters and 6 to 8 large chopped boiled shrimp. Cook only until edges of oysters curl and shrimp is hot.

You have deviled oysters and shrimp—a quick version of, and almost as good as, the original Louisiana recipe.

Serve over rice, or if you're in a real hurry, over toast.

Serves 4.

You could start with a well-made green salad and end with your best homemade custard.

Main-Course Recipes

Start with a first-course salad, then proceed to any of the following quick-cooking recipes, most of which are based on old-fashioned favorites. End the meal with fresh fruit and small wedges of cheese or crisp cookies and black coffee in small cups—a supper in double-quick time that is truly gourmet.

BAKED HAM AND TOMATO CHEESE FONDUE

1 1-pound can Italian-style tomatoes

2 cups soft bread crumbs from French- or Italian-style bread

1 medium onion, peeled and chopped

¼ pound crumbled cheddar cheese

¾ cup chopped baked or boiled ham

2 tablespoons butter

4 eggs, lightly beaten

1½ cups milk

¼ teaspoon dry mustard

½ teaspoon salt

¼ teaspoon pepper

4 to 6 dashes Tabasco sauce

Drain and chop tomatoes. Reserve juice.

Cover bottom of a well-greased casserole with bread crumbs. Cover with chopped tomatoes. Sprinkle with onion, cheese, and ham. Dot with slivers of butter. Repeat until all bread, tomatoes, onion, cheese, and ham have been used.

Combine reserved tomato juice and remaining ingredients. Beat with a wire whisk until well blended. Pour over bread, tomato, and cheese mixture in casserole.

Bake in a preheated 350° oven until firm, about 45 minutes.

Serves 6.

GLAZED HAM WITH CHERRIES

Glazed and tender, this is a very special ham casserole.

1 2-pound ready-to-eat ham steak
2 tablespoons honey
½ cup water
½ cup champagne (substitute dry white wine, apple cider, or apple juice)

¼ cup sugar
1 cup (canned) pitted black Bing cherries
Juice from 1 orange

Place ham in an oven casserole (one that may be used on top of the stove).* Add the honey and water. Place over low heat, and let simmer until all liquid has evaporated. Then add the remaining ingredients. Cover and place in a preheated 350° oven for 20 to 25 minutes.

Serve with fluffy white rice or, if you wish, baked sweet potatoes or yams.

Serves 4.

BASIC MEAT LOAF

2 pounds ground beef
1 cup soft bread crumbs
1 small white onion, peeled and finely minced
2 eggs, beaten
¾ cup Beef Stock (pages 22–23)
¼ cup dry red wine

3 tablespoons melted butter
3 tablespoons tomato puree
1 tablespoon salt
¼ teaspoon freshly ground black pepper
Butter
Spicy Meat-Loaf Glaze (page 52)

Combine all ingredients except butter and glaze. Blend well.

Butter an 8 by 4–inch loaf pan. Line bottom and sides with aluminum foil, letting foil extend over sides. Butter the foil. Fill pan with

---

* Enameled cast iron is one of the best types of casserole to use when you want to cook a dish first on top of the stove, then in the oven. However, if you do not have such a casserole, you may simmer the ham in a frypan, then transfer it to any baking dish with a cover.

meat-loaf mixture. Bake in a preheated 350° oven for 30 minutes. Continue to bake for another 30 minutes, basting with glaze every 8 to 10 minutes.

If you would be extra fancy, place pineapple rings on the top of your loaf about 10 minutes before it is ready to remove from the oven, and baste them with the glaze 3 or 4 times.

Lift from pan to serving platter, and let stand about 5 minutes before slicing.

Serves 6 to 8.

SPICY MEAT-LOAF GLAZE

¾ cup brown sugar, packed down   2 tablespoons dry mustard
2 tablespoons vinegar   ¾ cup water

Place all ingredients in a saucepan, and stir over low heat until sugar has dissolved. Bring to boil without stirring. Remove from heat, and let cool slightly before using.

STIR-FRIED CORNED BEEF AND CABBAGE

1 tablespoon oil   ½ teaspoon salt
2 tablespoons butter   1 pound cooked corned beef,
1 small cabbage, shredded   thinly sliced
2 tablespoons water

Heat oil and butter in a large heavy skillet. Add cabbage, and stir-fry for 1 minute. Add water, and sprinkle with salt. Cover and steam for 5 to 6 minutes or until cabbage is crisp-tender. Stir in corned beef slices, and continue to cook only until meat is heated.

Serves 4.

STIR-FRIED ORIENTAL BEEF AND MIXED VEGETABLES

1 pound top round of beef
2 tablespoons oil
2 medium carrots, scraped
2 stalks celery
2 or 3 small white onions, peeled and chopped
1 turnip, peeled and thinly sliced, each slice quartered
1 5-ounce can water chestnuts, drained and thinly sliced

3 tablespoons Beef Stock (pages 22–23) or water
½ pound spinach
2 to 3 tablespoons soy sauce or more if desired
Freshly ground black pepper
Salt if desired
Cooked rice
Chinese (canned) fried noodles

Have your butcher cut the beef into paper-thin slices. He can do this easily by first chilling the meat, then using the electric slicer he normally uses to slice cold cuts.

Heat the oil in a large heavy skillet with a tight-fitting lid. Add the meat, and cook, stirring and turning each piece until no longer pink.

Cut carrots at a 45° angle into thin oval slices. Cut celery in the same fashion into ½-inch lengths. Add carrots, celery, onions turnip, and water chestnuts to skillet. Stir-fry until all vegetables are coated with oil, then add stock or water, stir to blend, and cover and steam until vegetables are crisp-tender (about 3 minutes if you have sliced all vegetables very thinly or chopped them). Stir in spinach and soy sauce. Cover skillet once more, and steam for 1 minute or until spinach is wilted but still bright green. Season with pepper. Taste, and add salt if desired.

Spoon over cooked rice, and sprinkle each serving with crisp Chinese noodles. Pass additional soy sauce at the table.

Serves 4.

COMPANY HASH

3 tablespoons butter
2 tablespoons flour
1 cup milk
1 cup Chicken Stock (pages 23–24)
¼ cup dry sherry
¼ teaspoon salt

¼ teaspoon white pepper
2 egg yolks, beaten
1½ cups diced smoked turkey
1½ cups diced boiled or baked ham
½ cup cream, whipped
¼ cup grated Swiss cheese

Melt the butter in a deep heavy skillet (one that may be transferred to the oven). Stir in the flour, and cook, stirring, until well blended. Slowly add the milk, stirring as it is added. Add the stock and sherry. Continue to cook until mixture thickens. Remove from heat, and season with salt and pepper. Then quickly stir in egg yolks, and blend well. Add the turkey and ham. Cover with the whipped cream. Sprinkle with cheese. Place in a preheated 350° oven, and bake until surface is browned.

Serves 6.

You might present this gem of a hash on toasted English muffins. Peach halves filled with marmalade and then baked until steamy make this an epicurean supper.

STIR-FRIED PORK AND BEANS

1 pound boneless pork	1 1-pound jar or can imported flageolets (small white beans)
2 tablespoons oil	
1 tablespoon butter	3 to 4 tablespoons (bottled) Escoffier Sauce Robert
¼ cup Cognac or other good brandy	
	⅓ teaspoon freshly ground black pepper
2 small white onions, peeled and chopped	
	½ teaspoon salt
2 tablespoons Beef Stock (pages 22–23) or water	2 to 3 sprigs parsley, chopped
	Cooked rice

Cut pork in matchlike pieces. Heat the oil and butter in a heavy skillet. Add the pork, and stir-fry until lightly browned. Add Cognac and ignite. Remove skillet from heat until flame goes out.

Add onions and stock or water. Cover skillet, and let meat steam over medium heat for 5 to 6 minutes. Add flageolets, stir to blend, and cook until heated. Stir in Escoffier sauce. Season with pepper and salt. Stir in parsley.

Cook a final half minute, and serve over just-cooked hot rice.

Serves 4.

GROUND BEEF AND ZUCCHINI

2 tablespoons oil
1 pound ground top round
1 medium onion, peeled and
   chopped
1 small green pepper, seeded and
   cut into thin strips
3 medium zucchini, trimmed and
   thinly sliced
1 teaspoon ground ginger
2 tablespoons water

1 tablespoon cornstarch
2 tablespoons Beef or Chicken
   Stock (pages 22–24), water, or
   dry sherry
3 tablespoons soy sauce
Freshly ground black pepper
Salt if desired
Cooked rice
Chinese (canned) fried noodles

Heat the oil in a large heavy skillet, add meat, and cook, stirring, until no longer pink.

Add onion, green pepper, and zucchini. Stir-fry until vegetables are coated with oil. Sprinkle with ginger, and add water. Cover and steam until zucchini are crisp-tender.

Mix cornstarch and stock, water, or sherry. Stir into the skillet the soy sauce and the cornstarch mixture. Sprinkle with pepper, and cook, stirring, until sauce thickens. Taste, and add salt if desired.

Spoon over cooked rice, and sprinkle with Chinese noodles.

Serves 4.

Here are three double-quick-time veal recipes from three different countries of Europe. They are all made from thin slices of veal pounded even thinner by your butcher or by you. Called *scaloppine* by the Italians, *escalopes de veau* by the French, and *Wiener Schnitzel* by the Austrians, they are still and all cut in the same manner and from the same cut of meat.

ESCALOPES DE VEAU

8 veal scallops (1 pound)
Salt
Pepper
4 tablespoons butter
2 teaspoons flour

1 cup light cream
½ cup port wine
1 small can sautéed-in-butter
   mushroom slices

Place the veal scallops between waxed paper, and pound thin with a mallet or a rolling pin, or have your butcher do this for you.

Season each scallop with salt and pepper.

Heat 3 tablespoons of the butter in a large heavy skillet, add the scallops, and brown them lightly on both sides. Transfer to a heated platter.

Add remaining butter to the skillet. When melted, stir in the flour, and blend well. Remove pan from heat, and slowly add about half the cream, stirring as it is added. Return to heat, and add remaining cream and port wine. Cook, stirring, until sauce begins to thicken. Add mushrooms. Correct seasoning with additional salt and pepper, and continue to cook, stirring, until sauce is thick and smooth. Pour over veal, and serve with rice, noodles, or simply with good crusty bread.

Serves 4.

HUNGARIAN PAPRIKA CREAM SCHNITZEL

8 slices of boneless veal, 4 ounces
   each
2 tablespoons butter
1 tablespoon oil
1 small white onion, peeled and
   chopped

1 teaspoon sweet Hungarian
   paprika
Salt
1 cup sour cream
1 tablespoon tomato puree

Place the veal slices between pieces of waxed paper, and pound them thin with a mallet or a rolling pin, or have your butcher do this for you.

Heat the butter and oil in a large heavy skillet. Add the veal slices, and brown them on both sides. Add the chopped onion, and cook, stirring, until lightly browned. Pour off excess oil, and season meat with paprika and salt. Stir in the sour cream and tomato puree. Cover and let barely simmer over low heat for 15 minutes.

Serve with rice or flat noodles.

Serves 4.

VEAL SCALLOPINI NORTH ITALIAN STYLE

1 pound leg of veal, cut into 12 scallops
1½ cups fine dry bread crumbs
½ teaspoon salt
¼ teaspoon freshly ground black pepper
⅛ teaspoon paprika
⅛ teaspoon cayenne pepper
½ cup grated Parmesan cheese
2 eggs beaten with 1 tablespoon cold water
1 tablespoon oil

3 tablespoons butter
¼ pound fresh mushrooms, chopped
1 small white onion, peeled and chopped
1 8-ounce can Italian-style tomato sauce
¼ cup dry vermouth
¼ pound prosciutto ham, cut into narrow strips
4 thin slices mozzarella cheese

Have your butcher pound each scallop as thinly as possible.

Combine the bread crumbs, salt, pepper, paprika, cayenne pepper, and Parmesan cheese.

Dip each veal scallop first in beaten egg, then in bread-crumb mixture. Press crumbs firmly into each scallop.

Place the oil and 2 tablespoons of the butter in a heavy skillet over medium heat. When it starts to sizzle, add the scallops, and brown them quickly on both sides. Remove from skillet, and place scallops in a single layer on a double-thick sheet of foil. Place in a preheated 200° oven to keep warm while preparing sauce.

Add remaining butter to the skillet. Add the mushrooms and onion, and sauté until onion is limp. Pour in tomato sauce and vermouth. Stir to blend, and add ham. Cook, stirring frequently, over low heat for 4 to 5 minutes.

Return the scallops to the skillet, and spoon sauce over them. Place cheese over meat. Cover skillet, and place it in a preheated 325° oven. Bake until cheese has melted.

Flat noodles are the perfect go-with.

Serves 4.

Bifteck, Steaks, and Chops

Steaks or chops accompanied by rice or potatoes and a vegetable or salad are still first choice on American tables, but what to do with this Tuesday's lamb chops that will be different from last Sunday's? Isn't there some new and enticing way to serve a steak, and what about those supermarket special-priced pork chops? It's a problem, and even the best of cooks will sometimes run out of ideas.

The double-quick-time cook takes a tip from professional chefs: Panbroil these meats, and serve them with a garnish and a quick-cooking sauce that will enhance their flavor.

The French word for ground-meat patties is *bifteck*. Sounds elegant, and it is when prepared in the recipes that follow. What's more, they are no more trouble to prepare than plain old hamburgers. And (don't take my word for it, but just try them) they are really much more delicious.

BIFTECK MADEIRA

1 pound ground beef	2 tablespoons butter
½ cup Madeira	1 8-ounce can tomato sauce
1 clove garlic, peeled	2 cups cooked rice
Salt	¼ cup chopped parsley
Freshly ground black pepper	4 rolled anchovy fillets

Shape beef into 4 patties, place in a shallow nonmetal pan, and pour Madeira over them. Add garlic, and let stand at room temperature 1 hour. Turn patties occasionally.

Remove meat from Madeira, pat dry, and sprinkle with salt and pepper. Discard garlic, but reserve remaining Madeira.

Heat the butter in a heavy skillet. When it starts to brown, add patties, and cook, turning once to desired degree of rareness. Transfer to a warm serving platter. Keep warm.

Add the tomato sauce and the reserved Madeira to the juice in the pan, and cook, stirring, 4 to 5 minutes.

Surround beef patties with just-cooked hot rice. Pour sauce over both. Sprinkle with parsley, and top each meat patty with a rolled anchovy fillet.

Serves 4.

BIFTECK À LA RUSSE

1½ pounds ground beef	Flour (approximately ¼ cup)
2 tablespoons heavy cream	4 tablespoons butter
2 tablespoons grated onion	1 large onion, peeled, sliced, and
2 tablespoons minced parsley	broken into rings
1¼ teaspoons salt	3 tablespoons sour cream
½ teaspoon freshly ground black pepper	1 tablespoon (bottled) Escoffier Sauce Diane
¼ teaspoon paprika	Paprika
⅛ teaspoon nutmeg	

Mix together the beef, cream, onion, parsley, salt, pepper, paprika, and nutmeg. Form into 6 or 8 patties. Dredge each lightly with flour.

Heat 2 tablespoons of the butter in a heavy skillet. Add the onion rings, and sauté until lightly golden in color. Remove and keep warm.

Wipe skillet clean with paper toweling, return it to the heat, and add the remaining butter. When butter begins to brown, add the meat patties, and cook to desired degree of rareness, turning once.

Transfer meat to a heated platter, and top with sautéed onions.

Add the cream to the pan juices in the skillet, and stir to blend. Stir in the Sauce Diane. Cook, stirring constantly, until sauce is well heated, but do not allow to boil.

Pour over meat and onions. Dust with paprika, and serve. Serves 6 to 8.

BIFTECK À L'ANDALUSE

If this recipe seems complicated on first reading, read it again, and you'll see how easy it really is. No other vegetable is needed. Add rice or rice pilaf, and the meal is prepared.

2 small to medium tomatoes	Flour
1 small eggplant	2 tablespoons olive oil
2 tablespoons salt	1 small clove garlic, peeled
1 pound ground beef	3 tablespoons butter
2 tablespoons heavy cream	½ cup Beef Stock (pages 22–23)
1 teaspoon salt	Plain Boiled Rice or Rice Pilaf
½ teaspoon finely ground black pepper	(pages 76–78)

Cut tomatoes into 4 thick slices, discarding end pieces. Refrigerate until ready to cook.

Peel eggplant. Cut 4 ½-inch-thick slices from the center. Coarsely chop remaining end pieces. Sprinkle slices and chopped pieces with salt on all sides. Let stand at room temperature 25 to 30 minutes.

Mix together the beef, cream, and salt and pepper. Form into 4 patties.

Drain the eggplant slices, and pat dry. Dredge lightly with flour.

Heat the oil with the garlic in a heavy skillet over medium heat. Add the eggplant slices and the chopped eggplant, and cook until lightly browned. Remove from skillet, and keep warm.

Add 1 tablespoon of the butter to the skillet, and in it sauté the tomato slices for 5 minutes, turning once. Remove from skillet, and keep warm.

Remove garlic and oil from skillet, and wipe it clean with paper toweling. Return skillet to heat, and add the remaining butter. When it starts to brown, add the meat patties and cook to the desired degree of rareness, turning once.

Place 1 patty on each slice of eggplant, and top with tomato slice.

Add the stock to the pan juices in the skillet, and cook, stirring, over high heat until reduced by half. Pour over the meat and vegetables.

Mix sautéed chopped eggplant with just-cooked hot rice or rice pilaf. Serve as accompaniment to meat.

Serves 4.

TOURNEDOS À LA NIÇOISE

This is a more expensive dish than the preceding ones, but it is doubly delicious.

6 fillets of beef, cut 1 inch thick	⅛ teaspoon chervil
1½ teaspoons salt	½ teaspoon salt
½ teaspoon freshly ground black pepper	¼ teaspoon coarsely ground black pepper
1 tablespoon oil	6 slices white bread
5 tablespoons butter	½ cup dry white wine
4 medium tomatoes, chopped	1 tablespoon tomato puree
1 small clove garlic, peeled and minced	1 cup coarsely chopped black olives
⅛ teaspoon tarragon	

Have the fillets trimmed of fat and tied into neat rounds. Sprinkle with salt and pepper. Rub with oil, and let stand at room temperature for 1 hour.

Melt 2 tablespoons of the butter in a saucepan. Add the tomatoes, garlic, tarragon, chervil, and salt and pepper, and cook, stirring often, over low heat. Chop the tomatoes still more as they cook. Let simmer until reduced to a thick sauce, about 30 minutes. Keep warm.

Remove the crust from the bread slices, and cut them into rounds a little larger than the fillets.

Heat 1 tablespoon of the butter in a heavy skillet. In it sauté the bread rounds until lightly browned on both sides. Remove and keep warm in a 200° oven.

Wipe the skillet clean with paper toweling. Return it to a medium heat, and add the remaining butter. When butter starts to turn brown, add the fillets, and cook to the desired degree of rareness. Place one fillet on each sautéed bread round, and arrange on a warm platter.

Add the warm tomato sauce, the wine, and the tomato puree to the pan juices in the skillet, and cook, stirring, until sauce thickens. Stir in the chopped olives, and pour sauce over fillets. Serve with parslied new potatoes.

Serves 6.

LAMB CHOPS FLAMBÉS

This is for the showman cook—party fare, dramatic, and utterly superb.

8 loin lamb chops, cut 1½ inches
   thick
1 clove garlic, peeled and split
Salt
Freshly ground black pepper
8 apricot halves

1 tablespoon butter
½ cup (bottled) Cumberland
   sauce
¼ cup Cognac or other good
   brandy

Remove a little of the fat from each lamb chop, and cut it into small dice. Place it in a heavy skillet over medium heat. Stir until the bottom of the skillet is shiny with fat. Remove and discard dice. Turn heat to high, add the chops to the skillet, and brown them quickly on both sides. Lower heat, add garlic to skillet, and let chops cook to desired degree of rareness. Sprinkle with salt and pepper. Pour off fat as it accumulates in the pan.

While chops cook, place apricots and butter in a small saucepan over moderate heat. Turn them occasionally. Cook only until well heated.

Heat Cumberland sauce in the top half of a double boiler over simmering water.

To serve, transfer chops from skillet to a warm heatproof platter. Pour Cumberland sauce over chops. Surround with apricot halves. Heat

Cognac in a small skillet, ignite, and pour flaming over chops. Bring flaming platter to the table.

Serves 4.

LAMB CHOPS À L'ANGLAISE

You'll need an especially good—and willing—butcher for this recipe, but it's well worth the effort to find him for this dish alone.

6 loin lamb chops, about ⅓ inch thick	½ teaspoon salt
6 small thin slices of baked or boiled ham	½ teaspoon freshly ground black pepper
2 eggs, beaten with 1 tablespoon oil	¼ teaspoon cayenne pepper
1 cup fine dry bread crumbs made from day-old French or Italian bread	¼ teaspoon paprika
	4 tablespoons butter
	1 tablespoon lemon juice

Have your butcher remove all fat from the chops, then pound the meat as thinly as possible without removing meat from the bone.

Let chops stand at room temperature for 1 hour.

Cut ham into pieces just a little smaller than the center meat of the chops.

Dip chops in beaten egg, and cover meat part of chops with ham, pressing tightly together. Dip once more in egg, then in bread crumbs seasoned with salt, black pepper, cayenne pepper, and paprika. Press crumbs firmly into chops.

Place on rack, and let stand at room temperature 10 to 15 minutes.

Melt 3 tablespoons of the butter in a heavy skillet over medium heat. When butter sizzles, add the chops, and cook, turning once, until nicely browned on both sides. Transfer to a heatproof platter, and place in a 350° oven for 5 to 8 minutes.

Add the remaining butter and lemon juice to the pan juices in the skillet, and stir to blend. Pour over chops, and serve.

Fresh steamed green beans and the smallest of new potatoes dressed with butter and parsley would go well with this dish.

Serves 6.

CÔTES DE VEAU SAUTÉES BASQUAISE
(Sautéed Veal Chops Basque Style)

4 large veal chops, loin or rib
Salt
Pepper
2 tablespoons olive oil
3 tablespoons butter
2 small white onions, peeled and chopped
½ small green pepper, seeded and chopped
1 large ripe tomato, seeded and chopped
2 thin slices Bayonne or other smoked ham, cut into narrow strips
¼ cup Cognac
¼ cup dry white wine

Have the chops trimmed of all fat. Rub salt and pepper into both sides of each chop.

Heat the oil and butter in a heavy skillet. Add chops, and brown them on both sides. Cover and simmer for 20 to 25 minutes until tender.

Remove chops to a warm serving platter. Add the onion, green pepper, tomato, and ham to the pan, and cook, stirring, until onion and green pepper are soft. Pour in the Cognac and wine, and continue to cook, stirring, until sauce is reduced by about one third. Correct seasoning with additional salt and pepper as needed. Ladle sauce over chops, and serve at once.

Serves 4.

PORK CHOPS IN SOUR-CREAM SAUCE

8 loin pork chops, cut ½ inch thick
2 tart apples, peeled, cored, and cut in 1-inch slices
2 tablespoons lemon juice
Flour
1 teaspoon salt
½ teaspoon freshly ground black pepper
2 tablespoons Beef Stock (pages 22–23) or water
1 clove garlic, peeled and split
2 tablespoons butter
⅓ cup brown sugar
¾ cup sour cream
¼ cup seedless raisins

Trim some of the fat from the chops, and cut it into small dice.
Sprinkle apple slices with lemon juice, and dust lightly with flour.

Place diced fat in a heavy skillet over low heat, and cook, stirring occasionally, until the bottom of the skillet is coated with a thin layer of rendered fat.

Turn heat to high, add chops, and brown them quickly on both sides. Reduce heat to moderate. Sprinkle chops with salt and pepper, pour stock or water into skillet, and add garlic. Cover and cook chops for fifteen minutes. Turn them occasionally. (*Chops can be made ahead to this point. Reheat before continuing.*)

Remove chops from skillet, and keep warm. Discard garlic and diced fat. Pour off and discard cooking juices. Wipe pan clean with paper toweling.

Melt butter in skillet, add apple slices, and cook until lightly browned on both sides.

Return chops to skillet, place an apple slice on each, and sprinkle each with brown sugar. Pour in sour cream, and add raisins.

Cover skillet, and place it in a preheated 325° oven. Bake 15 to 20 minutes or until chops are tender.

Serves 4.

PORK CHOPS À LA GASCONNE

4 loin pork chops, cut 1½ inches thick	⅛ teaspoon thyme
1 clove garlic, peeled	½ cup dry white wine
¼ cup oil	½ cup pitted black olives, chopped
2 tablespoons vinegar	1 tablespoon (bottled) Escoffier Sauce Robert
1½ teaspoons salt	
½ teaspoon freshly ground black pepper	

Trim the fat from the chops, and cut it into small dice.

Cut the garlic in paper-thin slivers. With a small sharp knife insert one sliver of garlic deep into the meat of each chop.

Combine the oil, vinegar, salt, pepper, and thyme. Rub mixture well into each chop. Let stand at room temperature 1 hour.

Place the diced pork fat in a heavy skillet over moderate heat, and cook, stirring occasionally, until sufficient fat has been rendered to coat bottom of skillet. Remove and discard dice.

Add the chops to the skillet, and brown them quickly on both sides. Add ¼ cup of the wine. Cover skillet, and cook chops over low heat until very tender, about 30 minutes. (*Chops can be made ahead to this point. Reheat before continuing.*)

Transfer chops to a heated serving platter, and keep warm.

Add to skillet the remaining wine and the olives. Cook over fairly high heat until liquid is reduced by about half. Stir in the Escoffier Sauce Robert, and cook a final half minute.

Pour sauce over chops, and serve.

Serves 4.

Continental Chicken Dishes

CHINESE CHICKEN BREASTS WITH SNOW PEAS AND ALMONDS

1 10-ounce package frozen snow peas
2 whole chicken breasts, skinned and boned
1 teaspoon cornstarch
¼ cup dry sherry
2 tablespoons oil

3 tablespoons Chicken Stock (pages 23–24) or water
½ cup blanched slivered almonds
2 to 3 tablespoons soy sauce
Salt and pepper as needed
Cooked rice or flat noodles

Remove frozen snow peas from package, and let thaw at room temperature for 30 minutes. Pat thoroughly dry with paper toweling.

Cut chicken breast into bite-size cubes, and place in a nonmetal bowl.

Mix cornstarch with sherry, and pour over chicken. Let stand at room temperature for 30 minutes. Stir occasionally.

Heat the oil in a heavy skillet. Add chicken, and cook, stirring, until each piece is white.

Add snow peas to skillet, and stir until coated with oil. Add chicken stock or water, cover, and steam until crisp-tender, about 1 minute.

Add almonds and soy sauce. Cook, stirring, a final half minute. Taste, and add salt and pepper as needed.

Serve over steamy hot cooked rice or flat noodles.

Serves 4.

CHICKEN BREASTS LOUISE

For an elegant but carefree dinner party nothing tops these quick-to-make, prepared-ahead breasts of chicken stuffed with spicy Italian ham and melt-in-your-mouth cheese. The sauce can be made ahead, too.

3 whole chicken breasts
6 small thin slices of prosciutto ham
2 thin slices Swiss cheese
1 tablespoon butter
2 eggs, beaten with 1 tablespoon oil
1½ cups fine dry bread crumbs
½ teaspoon salt
½ teaspoon freshly ground black pepper
¼ teaspoon paprika
Tomato Mushroom Sauce (page 68)

Have your butcher skin and bone the chicken breasts. Cut each in half, place between two sheets of waxed paper, and pound thin.

Cover each halved breast with a slightly smaller slice of prosciutto, and place a strip of cheese on each slice of ham. Dot with slivers of butter. Roll up jelly-roll fashion, tucking in ends of chicken pieces as they are rolled. Press together firmly.

Dip each roll in beaten egg, then roll in the bread crumbs, which have been mixed with salt, pepper, and paprika. Repeat so that rolls are lightly but completely encased in crumbs.

Place rolls, not touching, on a rack, and refrigerate until well chilled.

Place, not touching, on a double-thick sheet of foil or on a baking sheet. Bake in a preheated 350° oven for 45 minutes.

Serve with Tomato Mushroom Sauce spooned over each roll or with Thick White Sauce (page 107).

Serves 6.

TOMATO MUSHROOM SAUCE

1 tablespoon butter
2 teaspoons flour
1 8-ounce can Italian-style tomatoes
1 4-ounce can sautéed-in-butter mushrooms
⅓ cup dry white wine
Salt
Pepper

Melt butter in a heavy saucepan. When bubbly, stir in flour, and blend until smooth. Add tomatoes, mushrooms, and wine. Season lightly with salt and pepper to taste, and cook, stirring, over low heat until sauce thickens.

FRIED-IN-THE-OVEN CHICKEN WITH MUSHROOM GRAVY

Broiled peach halves are just dandy with this wonderful new-style old-style dish.

1 broiler-fryer chicken, 2 to 2½ pounds
Salt
Pepper
2 tablespoons butter
½ cup chopped fresh mushrooms
2 tablespoons flour
1 cup milk
½ cup Chicken Stock (pages 23–24)

Have your butcher cut the broiler-fryer into serving pieces. Wash each piece under cold running water. Blot thoroughly dry with paper toweling, and let stand 30 minutes at room temperature.

Place pieces skin side up, not touching, in a large shallow enamelized cast-iron pan (or similar baking dish that may also be used over direct heat). Place in a preheated 350° oven, and bake for 45 minutes. Sprinkle with salt and pepper, and continue to bake for 15 minutes or until chicken is tender and each piece is well browned.

Remove pan from oven, and transfer chicken pieces to a warm plate. Pour all chicken fat from pan, and add butter. Place over moderate heat. When butter has melted, add mushrooms, and cook, stirring, for a half minute. Sprinkle with flour, and stir a second half minute, then slowly add milk and stock, stirring as they are added. Continue to cook and stir until gravy is smooth and has started to thicken. Season lightly with salt and pepper. Return pieces to pan, and baste with gravy. Place pan in oven once again, and cook a final 10 to 15 minutes, basting chicken with gravy frequently as it bakes.

Serves 4.

STUFFED CHICKEN BREASTS WITH PÂTÉ AND TRUFFLES

3 whole chicken breasts	1½ cups fine dry bread crumbs
1 small can pâté	½ teaspoon salt
1 small can sliced truffles	¼ teaspoon freshly ground black
2 tablespoons butter	pepper
2 eggs, beaten with 1 tablespoon oil	¼ teaspoon paprika
	White Sauce (pages 106–107)

Have your butcher skin and bone the chicken breasts. Cut each in half, place between two sheets of waxed paper, and pound thin.

Spread each halved breast with pâté, and top with 2 or 3 slices of truffles. Dot with slivers of butter. Roll up jelly-roll fashion, tucking in ends of chicken pieces as they are rolled to make a neat little loaf. Press edges together firmly.

Dip each roll in beaten egg, then roll in the bread crumbs, which have been seasoned with salt, pepper, and paprika. Repeat so that rolls are lightly but completely encased in crumbs.

Arrange seam side down and not touching on a rack. Refrigerate until chilled.

Place on foil or baking sheet, and bake in a preheated 350° oven for 45 minutes.

Serve with any good rich white sauce spooned over each roll.

Serves 6.

CHICKEN IN CHAMPAGNE SAUCE

1 3½-pound frying chicken, cut into serving pieces
Salt
¼ pound butter
½ pound mushrooms, chopped
½ pound shallots, peeled and chopped
⅓ cup Cognac or other good brandy
1 cup champagne
¼ cup Chicken Stock (pages 23–24)
2 tablespoons heavy cream
Salt
Pepper

Sprinkle chicken pieces with salt.

Melt the butter in a deep heavy skillet, and add the chicken pieces. Cook over low heat, turning often, until chicken is golden on all sides. Add the mushrooms and shallots, and cook, stirring, until shallots are soft. Pour the Cognac over the chicken, and ignite it. When the flame dies out, add the champagne and stock. Cover and cook over low heat until chicken is very tender, about 45 minutes.

Remove chicken to a warm serving platter.

Add the cream to the skillet, and cook, stirring, over low heat until liquid is reduced by about half. Correct seasoning with salt and pepper. Pour over chicken, and serve.

Serves 4.

Fish International

To avoid kitchen panic and/or overcooked fish, Chef Rene Scanlon of the Waldorf Astoria says:

"There are only two ways to go about preparing a meal that features fish.

"One: Prepare fish or shellfish in sauce. Then prepare balance of meal. When everything is almost ready to take to the table, reheat your sauced dish.

"Or two: Prepare every other item on the menu, and keep warm. Then cook your fish or shellfish by any fast-cooking method.

"Either way you can give your undivided attention to this temperamental part of the meal."

Makes sense.

BAKED OYSTER-STUFFED FILLETS OF SOLE

6 fillets of sole
1 dozen oysters and their liquid
4 tablespoons butter
2 tablespoons flour
½ cup milk (approximately)
½ cup clam juice
¼ cup dry vermouth

½ teaspoon salt
¼ teaspoon white pepper
½ cup flaked crabmeat
2 tablespoons fine dry bread crumbs
1 tablespoon melted butter

Cut each fillet in half lengthwise. Drain oysters, reserving liquid. Wrap a halved fillet around each oyster, and secure with a toothpick.

Melt 2 tablespoons of the butter in a heavy skillet over moderate heat. Add the oyster-stuffed fillets, and sauté until fish becomes opaque. Transfer them to a shallow baking dish.

Pour cooking liquid from the skillet, and wipe clean with paper toweling. Return the skillet to moderate heat, and add the remaining butter. When butter has melted, add the flour, and stir until mixture is smooth. Slowly add the milk, stirring as it is added. Add clam juice, oyster liquid, vermouth, and salt and pepper. Cook, stirring, until sauce thickens. Stir in the crabmeat, and pour over oyster-stuffed fillets.

Sprinkle with bread crumbs that have been mixed with the melted butter. (*The dish can be made ahead to this point.*)

Place in a preheated oven, and bake 10 to 15 minutes.

Plain boiled rice and pickled peaches make this a superb party dish. Serves 6.

DEVILED CRAB

Instead of crabmeat you may substitute chopped cooked shrimp, scallops, or lobster meat or combine any of these shellfish for Deviled Shellfish Supreme.

5 tablespoons butter
½ cup finely chopped fresh mushrooms
¼ cup finely chopped shallots
4 tablespoons flour
¾ cup milk
¼ cup dry white wine
¼ teaspoon salt
¼ teaspoon dry mustard

½ teaspoon Worcestershire sauce
Dash of Tabasco sauce
1 cup mayonnaise
1 tablespoon finely chopped pimiento
1 pound crabmeat
¾ cup fine dry bread crumbs
¼ cup melted butter

Melt 1 tablespoon of the butter in a heavy skillet. Add mushrooms and shallots, and cook, stirring, until shallots are limp. Transfer shallots and mushrooms to a small bowl. Set aside.

Melt remaining butter in skillet, and stir in flour. When well blended and smooth, slowly add milk, stirring as it is added. Add wine, salt, mustard, Worcestershire, and Tabasco. Cook, stirring, until sauce is thick and smooth. Remove from heat. Cool slightly, then add mayonnaise, and blend well. Fold in pimiento, crabmeat, and sautéed shallots and mushrooms. Pile into shells or into individual ramekins. Top with bread crumbs mixed with melted butter. (*The dish can be made ahead to this point.*) Bake in a preheated 425° oven only until lightly browned.

Serves 4 generously as a main course. Serves 6 as a first course, or you may spoon mixture into 8 or 10 of the smallest soufflé dishes available, and serve as a hot hors d'oeuvre.

SCALLOPED SCALLOPS

1½ pounds bay scallops
¼ teaspoon salt
20 salted crackers
½ cup melted butter

1 tablespoon minced chives
4 tablespoons light cream
Pepper
Paprika

Wash and drain scallops. Sprinkle with salt.

Crumble crackers, and mix with melted butter and chives.

Arrange alternate layers of cracker crumbs and scallops in a 9-inch greased pie plate, making 3 layers of crumbs and 2 layers of scallops. Pour cream over surface. Sprinkle with pepper and paprika.

Bake in a preheated 425° oven for 30 minutes.

Serves 4.

SALMON SOUFFLÉ

Here is a French version of a salmon loaf that is so elegant we'll call it a soufflé.

Butter
2 medium-size Idaho potatoes, peeled and chopped
3 large eggs
1 large ripe tomato, coarsely chopped
¼ cup milk

½ teaspoon salt
¼ teaspoon freshly ground black pepper
2 or 3 dashes each Tabasco and Worcestershire sauces
1 7½-ounce can salmon

Grease a 2-quart soufflé dish generously with butter.

Place potatoes, eggs, tomato, and milk in electric blender. Add salt, pepper, and Tabasco and Worcestershire sauces. Blend at high speed until mixture resembles very thick, smooth, and heavy cream.

Place salmon in a mixing bowl, and flake with a fork. Add the potato mixture, and blend well. Pour into well-buttered soufflé dish, and place in preheated 350° oven. Bake until firm, about 30 minutes.

Serve hot from the dish with a generous ladling of tiny green peas in Rich Cream Sauce (pages 107–108) over each serving.

Serves 4 to 6.

HONG KONG SHRIMP AND GREEN BEANS

1 10-ounce package frozen French-style green beans
½ cup oil
1 piece ginger root, peeled and chopped
1 medium onion, peeled and chopped
2 pounds fresh or frozen shrimp, peeled and deveined

8 to 10 (canned) water chestnuts, thinly sliced
3 tablespoons soy sauce
1 teaspoon sugar
2 tablespoons dry sherry
Salt and pepper to taste
Cooked rice
Chinese (canned) fried noodles

Remove frozen beans from package. Break up frozen block, and let thaw at room temperature, about 30 minutes. Pat thoroughly dry with paper toweling.

Heat oil in a heavy skillet. Add ginger and onion. Stir-fry for 1 minute. Add shrimp, and cook, stirring, for 3 minutes. Stir in green beans, and cook, stirring, a half minute. Pour off almost all oil. Add water chestnuts. Stir in soy sauce, sugar, and sherry. Cover and steam until green beans are tender. Taste, and season lightly with salt and pepper.

Spoon over just-cooked steamy hot rice. Sprinkle each serving with Chinese noodles.

Serves 4.

6

The Quick Cook's Way with Rice, Potatoes, and Pasta

Rice

First let's talk about rice—not the so-called instant, please, which just doesn't taste good, and what's more, despite the name, does not save time when preparing the total meal.

Easy-cooking and great-tasting converted long-grained rice, brown rice, and imported Italian rice are the subjects to be covered here. Their superior flavor and nutrition makes them well worth the small effort they take to prepare.

Which rice to cook? It's up to you and your preference.

Budget-priced brown rice is very nutritious. It has a nutlike flavor that is vaguely similar to that astronomically expensive grain called wild rice. To further this illusion, stir in about ½ cup slivered water chestnuts or pignolias (pine nuts) to cooked rice just before serving. A few currants or white raisins may be added at will.

Converted long-grained white rice, unlike plain white rice, is prepared by treating the unmilled rice with steam under pressure, so that all the B vitamins are retained. It cooks up beautifully—white and appetizing. To add eye appeal plus flavor, gently fork-stir in about ½ cup finely minced parsley or chives just before serving.

Imported short-and-plump-grained rice from the Piedmont section of Italy is the lowest-calorie rice. It is a staple item in most Italian grocery stores, and it may be purchased in the delicacy departments of many fine shops. When cooked, it is fluffy and dry but never dried out. The flavor is exceptional—so superb that your guests will ask for your recipe. It is also high in good nutrition. It is the absolute best rice for pilafs and baked rice dishes.

To start, here's a "never-fail" basic recipe for plain boiled rice, using any of these three kinds. The end result: rice that is fluffy and dry; never sticky, gummy, or completely dried out.

PLAIN BOILED RICE

Water: 3 cups for long-grained converted rice
5 cups for imported Italian rice
4 cups for brown rice

1 cup unwashed, converted long-grained white rice, brown rice, or imported Italian rice
¾ teaspoon salt
2 teaspoons oil, or 1 teaspoon oil and 1 teaspoon butter

Bring water to a full boil in a large pot with a tight-fitting lid.

Add rice slowly, a few grains at a time, so that water does not cease to boil. Add salt and oil. Let water remain at a full boil for about a half minute. This is important. At the boiling point the starchy part of the rice is quickly cooked, preventing it from soaking out to thicken the water and hold the grains together in a sticky, gummy mass.

If brown rice is used, skim surface until water is clear.

Lower heat, and let rice simmer very gently until tender and almost all water has been absorbed. This takes about 20 minutes. Do not stir.

If heat is too high and all water evaporates before rice is tender, add about ¼ cup boiling water, and continue to cook. Repeat if necessary.

When only about 1 tablespoon water remains and rice is tender, remove pan from heat, and immediately cover with tight-fitting lid.

Let stand 8 to 10 minutes on the back of the stove or in a warm 150° oven until rice is completely dry. Uncover to test for dryness only after 8 minutes.

And that's all there is to it except to serve and enjoy. As to that matter of time: Start your rice first, then let it cook while preparing the rest of the meal. Everything will be ready at once with not one minute lost.

Serves 4.

RICE PILAF

You're going to have an elegant supper party and absolutely everything from appetizers to liqueurs after espresso must be simply superb.

If the meal is to be "continental style" and rice is part of the menu, it follows that a pilaf is the rice dish to serve.

This version is easy to prepare, and it can be made ahead and then reheated, which is all to the good.

I promise you it will be delicious.

1 tablespoon oil	2 cups boiling water
4 tablespoons butter at room temperature	2½ cups boiling Chicken Stock (pages 23–24)
¼ cup shallots, finely chopped, or chopped little white onions	Salt
	Freshly ground black pepper
1 cup pignolias or slivered (canned) water chestnuts	2 tablespoons currants
	¼ cup dry sherry
2 cups imported Italian rice	½ cup dry white wine

Place oil with 3 tablespoons of the butter in a large saucepan over medium heat. When butter has melted, add shallots, pignolias, and rice. Cook, stirring, until each grain of rice is coated with the oil and butter, the shallots are soft, and the nuts have begun to take on a little brown color.

Now add all at once the boiling water, then the 2½ cups boiling stock, and let boil for 1 minute. Reduce heat so that liquid just barely simmers, and cook without stirring until almost all liquid has been absorbed. Season lightly with salt and pepper.

(At this point you may cover the pan, and leave it on the back of the stove for up to 2 hours, or you may cover and refrigerate up to 24 hours. Take from refrigerator 1 hour before proceeding.)

"Plump up" currants by soaking them in dry sherry for 15 to 20 minutes. Drain.

Add wine, the remaining 1 tablespoon of butter, and the currants, and continue to cook until all but about 1 tablespoon of liquid has been absorbed and rice is tender. Cover and place in a low 150° oven for 10 to 12 minutes or until rice is completely dry.

Serves 8 to 10.

For a main-course dish cook pilaf as directed, then add: ½ to 1 cup chopped boiled shrimp or ¼ to ½ pound leftover lean roast beef, pork, or lamb, cut into thin narrow strips.

PARTY RICE PILAF WITH GREEN PEAS

1 10-ounce package frozen green peas
4 tablespoons butter at room temperature
2 cups imported Italian rice
2 cups Chicken Stock (pages 23–24)
4 cups water
½ teaspoon salt
1 small white onion, peeled and chopped
4 stalks celery, chopped
2 pimientos, chopped
1 cup pignolias
6 to 8 dashes Worcestershire sauce
Salt
Pepper
Paprika

Remove frozen peas from package and place on a plate. Set aside. (The peas will have separated and be partially thawed by the time you are ready to use them.)

Melt 2 tablespoons of the butter in a large ovenproof casserole that may be used on top of the stove. Add the rice, and cook, stirring, over low heat until each grain of rice is coated with butter.

Combine chicken stock and water in a saucepan, bring to a boil, and pour over rice. Add salt, and stir once to blend. Let simmer over low heat until rice is tender and all but 2 tablespoons water has been absorbed, about 25 minutes.

Add the now partially thawed peas, the remaining butter, onion, celery, pimientos, and pignolias. Sprinkle surface with the Worcestershire sauce and salt, pepper, and paprika to taste. Gently lift and stir the mixture with a fork until ingredients are blended.

Cover casserole, and place in a preheated 350° oven. Bake 15 to 20 minutes or until peas are tender and pilaf is steamy hot.

Serves 8 to 10.

LEMON PARSLEY PILAF

2 tablespoons butter at room temperature
1 small white onion, chopped
1 cup long-grained rice
3 cups boiling water
½ to ¾ cup chopped parsley
Juice from ½ small lemon

Melt 1 tablespoon of the butter in a saucepan. Add the onion and rice. Cook, stirring, over low heat until onion is limp and each grain of rice is coated with butter.

Pour in the boiling water, and bring to a full boil, then lower heat, and let simmer until rice is tender and almost all water has been absorbed.

Add parsley, lemon juice, and the remaining butter. Stir gently with a fork to blend parsley with rice. Remove from heat. Cover pan, and let stand 8 to 10 minutes before serving.

Serves 4 to 6.

BROWN-RICE PILAF

To my way of thinking a pilaf of natural brown rice is as elegant and delicious as wild rice. It's only incidental that it costs considerably less.

Melt 2 tablespoons of butter in a large saucepan over low heat. Add 1 cup of natural brown rice plus 2 tablespoons of chopped onions. Stir until the onions are transparent, then add 4 cups clear chicken stock and a sprinkling of salt. Bring to a boil, and skim the surface with a large spoon until clear. Then let simmer until almost all the liquid has been absorbed. Gently stir in pignolias and currants—about a half cup of each will do nicely. Cover the pot, remove it from the heat, and let stand about 10 minutes before serving. You'll have fluffy—not sticky—brown rice.

Serves 4 to 6.

Potatoes

There are just plain baked potatoes, and then there are lovely, delicious, and superb baked potatoes. Here's how for the latter, which takes no more effort or time; it's just a matter of a few simple rules.

When baking more than one, select potatoes of uniform size, or someone will end up with his or hers over- or undercooked. The best are large mealy potatoes of the Idaho variety.

Preheat oven to 500°.

Wash each potato, and dry well. Then rub each with a good fresh and fragrant oil. Try sesame-seed oil—it's superb.

With a small sharp knife make a few slits in each potato. Place them on the middle rack of your preheated oven for 15 minutes, then turn the temperature down to 350°.

Let bake until soft. It takes 1 to 1½ hours, depending on size. Test by pressing the sides of the potatoes with your fingers, protected, of course, with a clean dishcloth. You'll have a potato that is mealy and soft inside with skin that is crisp and crackling good.

When done, split open with a sharp knife, then press ends to open still farther. Fill opening with a pat of butter, and sprinkle with salt. If you are a weight-watcher, have ready a small ball of cottage cheese and chives. To make these, mash cottage cheese until smooth, add a little grated Parmesan cheese, form into balls, and roll in finely minced chives. Don't refrigerate—use at room temperature.

DIET COLCANNON

Mashed potatoes are not too fattening. It's the butter and cream that add those pounds. Here's one good and tasty way to bypass ingredients prohibited to dieters.

8 medium potatoes	½ teaspoon salt or more if desired
½ cup milk	½ teaspoon freshly ground black
½ cup minced chives	pepper or less if preferred
1 cup cottage cheese	

Peel and dice the potatoes. Cook them in simmering salted water to cover until they are soft (15 to 20 minutes). Pour off water, and dry the potatoes by shaking the pan over the heat.

Meanwhile, as potatoes cook, combine the milk and chives in a double boiler, and cook over simmering water until steamy hot. Do not allow to boil. Add cottage cheese, and blend well. Keep hot over hot water until potatoes are cooked.

Place boiled hot potatoes in a large mixing bowl, and mash until smooth. Using a fork, gradually start beating in the hot cottage-cheese mixture. When all has been added, season with salt and pepper, and continue beating until mixture is light, fluffy, and smooth.

Serve at once.

Serves 6 to 8.

BAKED POTATOES AND ONIONS

4 medium potatoes, peeled and cut into paper-thin slices
1 large purple onion, peeled and cut into paper-thin slices
2 tablespoons butter

1 tablespoon chopped parsley
Salt
Pepper
1 cup Beef or Chicken Stock (pages 22–24)

Place a layer of potato slices in a shallow baking pan. Cover with a few onion slices. Dot with slivers of butter, and sprinkle with parsley and salt and pepper. Repeat until all ingredients are used, ending with potato slices.

Place stock in a small saucepan, and bring to a full boil. Pour over potato mixture.

Place in a preheated 400° oven, and bake until crusty brown on top, 30 to 35 minutes.

Serves 4 to 6.

OVEN-FRIED POTATOES

Here are potatoes that are less greasy, better tasting, and a lot less work to prepare than french fries.

Select large mealy potatoes of the Idaho variety. Scrub them clean, and cook in simmering water to cover for 15 minutes or until just barely tender.

Let cool. Peel and cut into uniform slices about ¼ inch thick.

Combine equal parts butter and vegetable oil. Heat until butter melts. Remove from heat. Dip slices in mixture, and place them in a single layer on a long cookie sheet or, better yet, on foil.

Place in a preheated 400° oven, and bake until lightly browned, about 10 minutes.

You can prepare sweet potatoes or yams in the same way. The results are very good—in fact, delicious.

NEW POTATOES STEAMED IN BUTTER

Boiled potatoes are just fine for potato salad, but if you are cooking new potatoes, they are far superior when butter-steamed.

12 small new potatoes	Salt
Chicken or Beef Stock (pages 22– 24)	Freshly ground black pepper
2 tablespoons butter	Chopped parsley or chives

Wash potatoes, and dry thoroughly. Do not peel.

Fill a large 9- or 10-inch enamelized cast-iron or other heavy pan with a tight-fitting lid with stock to a depth of about 1 inch. Add the potatoes and butter. Sprinkle lightly with salt. Cover and steam over low heat until potatoes are tender and almost all liquid has evaporated, about 30 minutes. Add a little more stock or butter if necessary but only a little. Potatoes should cook in the steam from the liquid, not boil in it.

Sprinkle with pepper and parsley or chives. Add additional salt if needed, and serve very hot.

Serves 4 to 6.

NEW POTATOES IN CHEESE

Steam new potatoes as in preceding recipe. When done, roll in grated Parmesan or Romano cheese, and serve at once.

Pasta

How to Cook Spaghetti

Use 3 quarts water for every 8 ounces (½ pound) spaghetti.

Bring water to a full rolling boil in a large pot—the larger, the better.

Add 1 teaspoon oil and 1 teaspoon salt for every 3 quarts water.

Lower spaghetti into boiling water a little at a time so that water continues to boil. This is important. If water ceases to boil, the strands of spaghetti will stick together and cook unevenly.

Let boil briskly—uncovered—for from 5 to 12 minutes, depending on thickness and type of spaghetti.

Start testing after 4 minutes. Lift up a strand, and bite into it. Repeat every minute until cooked *al dente*—in other words, not oversoft, but resilient and with no starchy taste.

As soon as spaghetti is cooked, remove the pot from the stove, and quickly pour it into a colander. Then, just as quickly, transfer it to warm serving plates or flat soup bowls, and serve at once—with or without hot sauce ladled over each serving. Or transfer spaghetti to a warm deep and large tureen, and quickly stir in bits of butter to keep the strands from sticking together. Bring to the table, and serve sauce separately.

Do not mix cooked spaghetti and hot sauce in the kitchen. There's a reason: The heat of the sauce will continue to cook the spaghetti before it is served.

Serve spaghetti, then ladle hot sauce over it, and let each person mix his or her own.

Cook macaroni and egg noodles or pasta of any kind in the same way.

For very fine noodles start testing for doneness after boiling 2 minutes.

You don't always have to serve pasta with a tomato sauce or for that matter any sauce.

If you buy the best-quality pasta—preferably imported from Italy—it is perfectly delicious served without a sauce as a separate or main course or as an accompaniment (instead of rice or potatoes) to meat, fowl, or fish.

Simply cook and drain spaghetti, macaroni, or any type of pasta, then quickly return it to the same still-hot pan in which it was cooked or into a warm large tureen or serving bowl, and add tiny slivers of butter plus a goodly amount of finely chopped fresh parsley, chives, or watercress—one or more—then toss lightly and serve. Or add slivers of butter plus plenty of grated Romano or Parmesan cheese and chopped parsley if you like. Or add butter plus pimiento slivers and cheese, or butter plus seeded and chopped ripe tomato.

If you have ever eaten in an Italian restaurant (and who hasn't?), you probably know about *fettuccine Alfredo*—that wonderful Roman concoction of noodles, butter, cream, and Parmesan cheese—but did you know that there are numerous versions of this dish and that you can use any one of them as an entrée for an easy but elegant Italian party meal?

Well, there are, and you can. Here's how to go about it.

Start your meal in the living room with a hearty (made-ahead) antipasto. Have all your main-dish ingredients ready and waiting in the dining room to prepare after your guests have assembled at the table. (Choose any one of the three recipes that follow.)

Then back to the living room once again for espresso served with Italian cookies (you can buy them) and perhaps a big bowl of fresh fruit.

Two of the following recipes were discovered on board the very Italian *Michelangelo* while sailing to Naples, and the third, aboard the *Rafaello* on my return trip. Those lovely Italians. I gained a few pounds, but I still love them.

SPAGHETTI ALLA FIORELLO*

1 1-pound package thin spaghetti
4 tablespoons butter at room temperature
4 ounces cooked tongue, cut into narrow strips
4 ounces Canadian bacon, cut into narrow strips
4 ounces prosciutto ham, cut into narrow strips

1 tablespoon A-1 Sauce (commercially bottled)
½ cup heavy cream
¼ teaspoon cayenne pepper
2 tablespoons grated Parmesan cheese
Salt
Pepper

Cook spaghetti according to package directions for *al dente* (just slightly undercooked). Drain and place in a heated bowl. Add 1 tablespoon of the butter, toss lightly, cover, and keep warm.

Place the remaining butter in a chafing dish over a medium flame (or in an electric skillet with temperature at 350°). When it has melted,

* "Fiorello" is Fiorello De Farolfi, chief purser aboard the *Michelangelo*.

add the tongue, bacon, and ham. Cook, stirring frequently, 2 to 3 minutes, then add the A-1 sauce and cream, and continue to cook, stirring, 1 to 2 minutes longer or until steamy hot. Add the spaghetti, cayenne pepper, and cheese. Remove pan from heat, and season with salt and pepper. Toss mixture lightly, ladle onto warm plates, and serve at once.

Serves 4.

NOODLES MICHELANGELO

1 1-pound package flat egg noodles
4 tablespoons butter at room temperature
¾ cup diced cooked turkey meat
¾ cup diced boiled or baked ham
½ cup chopped fresh mushrooms
2 tablespoons Cognac or other good brandy
¼ cup Marsala wine
¾ cup heavy cream
¼ cup grated Swiss cheese
2 tablespoons grated Parmesan cheese
Salt
Pepper
2 tablespoons minced parsley

Cook noodles according to package directions for *al dente* (slightly undercooked). Drain and place in a warm bowl. Add 1 tablespoon of the butter, and toss lightly. Cover and keep warm.

Place the remaining butter in a chafing dish over medium flame (or in an electric skillet with temperature at 350°). Add the turkey, ham, and mushrooms. Cook, stirring, 2 to 3 minutes, then add the Cognac and wine. Reduce heat, cover, and cook until liquid has reduced by about half. Stir in cream and cheeses. Season lightly with salt and pepper, and continue to cook, stirring, until mixture is steamy hot. Add parsley, and pour over noodles. Toss lightly and serve at once.

Serves 4.

FLAT NOODLES WITH CHEESE AND HAM

Here is a method of preparation that takes less time than baking, and the results are much more delicious.

1 1-pound package flat noodles
3 tablespoons butter
1 cup diced boiled or baked ham
1 cup ricotta cheese (or cottage cheese) at room temperature
¼ cup grated Parmesan cheese
¼ teaspoon freshly ground black pepper
Salt

Cook noodles according to package directions. Drain and place in a heated bowl. Add 1 tablespoon of the butter. Toss lightly, cover, and keep warm.

Place remaining butter in a chafing dish over a medium flame (or in an electric skillet with temperature at 350°). When it is melted, add the ham, and cook, stirring, until it is heated. Remove from heat, and stir in cheeses. Add pepper, and season lightly with salt. Pour over noodles. Toss and serve.

Serves 4.

SPAGHETTI WITH HOT-SAUSAGE SAUCE

This recipe starts in the kitchen, but it can be served in a chafing dish.

1 pound sweet Italian sausage	1 6-ounce can tomato paste
½ pound hot Italian sausage	½ teaspoon thyme
1 large (purple) Italian onion, peeled and chopped	1 teaspoon oregano
	Salt
1 small green pepper, seeded and chopped	Freshly ground black pepper
	1 1-pound package thin spaghetti
1 1-pound can imported Italian tomatoes with basil	

Place both sweet and hot sausage in a large heavy skillet, and cook until browned. Add onion and green pepper, and continue to cook, stirring often, until vegetables are tender. Add tomatoes, tomato paste, thyme, and oregano. Stir to blend, and season lightly with salt and pepper. Bring to boil, then lower heat, and let simmer very gently for 25 to 30 minutes.

Cook spaghetti according to package directions. Drain. Place in a large serving bowl. Add sauce, and serve.

Serves 4.

After this, espresso and thin slices of melon sprinkled with fresh lime juice are all that is needed or for that matter wanted.

Truck-Garden Fare—Vegetables Made Interesting

In the thirties "just open, heat, and eat" canned vegetables were the thing. Then, from the forties on, frozen vegetables were in. The sixties brought us ready-sauced vegetables in little drop-in-the-boiling-water bags. Tasteless, trite, expensive, and a delusion, perhaps they finally convinced us that fresh vegetables did not, after all, take that much effort to prepare and that the resulting fresh flavor was well worth the short extra time.

Steamed Vegetables

When properly prepared, steamed vegetables are vegetables as they should be—fresh as just picked, with sunshine and garden flavor intact. Preferably they should come from your own garden, but at least get them from the best greengrocer in town. Correctly prepared, they will retain most of their "just-picked" flavor, as well as almost all vitamin and mineral content.

Steam and serve them seasoned only with salt and pepper and perhaps a squeeze of fresh lemon juice and a small pat of sweet butter, or dress them grandly as in the recipes to follow.

87

How to Steam Vegetables

Wash vegetables thoroughly.

Steam greens such as spinach or kale in only the water that clings to their leaves. Scrape and slice or dice carrots. Separate cauliflower and broccoli into flowerets.

Asparagus should be tied into neat bundles with soft string. (If you do not have an asparagus steamer, the bottom half of a double boiler with the top reversed makes a very acceptable substitute.)

Fill pan with water to a depth of ½ to 1 inch, sprinkle with salt, and bring to boil. Add vegetables, cover, and steam over medium heat until crisp-tender. (Time depends on type of vegetable and how cut, but 5 to 10 minutes is usually all that is needed.) Do not overcook. If necessary, add a little more boiling water during cooking procedure, but only if the bottom of the pan becomes completely dry. There should be very little water when vegetable is done.

CARROTS VICHY

Steamed carrots are called carrots Vichy in French restaurants, and they are steamed in a rather elegant manner.

Scrape, then slice sufficient carrots (very thin rounds) to make 2 cups sliced carrots. Place them in a saucepan with 1 tablespoon of butter. Sprinkle with ½ teaspoon salt and a teaspoon of sugar. Add sufficient water to just barely cover. Bring to a riotous boil, then let simmer until water has evaporated. Add a second tablespoon of butter, the juice from half a lemon, and 2 tablespoons finely chopped parsley. Cook, stirring, until carrots are well glazed.

Serves 4 to 6.

STEAMED CARROTS WITH HONEY AND FRESH MINT

A sprinkling of chopped fresh mint over almost any steamed vegetable makes a rare contribution. Serve the vegetable soon after adding the chopped mint. If allowed to cook more than a few moments, the mint tends to become bitter.

⅓ cup water
Salt
  6 to 8 medium carrots, scraped
    and very thinly sliced (about 2
    cups sliced carrots)

2 tablespoons honey
1 tablespoon butter
¼ cup chopped fresh mint

Bring water to boil, and sprinkle lightly with salt. Add carrots, cover, and steam until tender. Drain off water. Add honey and butter. Stir until butter has melted. Add mint, stir to blend, and correct seasoning with salt as needed.

Serves 4 to 6.

STEAMED ZUCCHINI

Zucchini, of the squash family, is a vegetable to be counted on. Its mild but distinctive flavor is liked by almost all. The absolutely easiest way to cook it is to steam it in foil.

Dice 2 large or 3 medium zucchini, leaving the skin on. Place the dice on a large square of heavy-duty foil. Add a small peeled and chopped white onion and 1 teaspoon each of butter, lemon juice, and water. Sprinkle with salt and freshly ground black pepper. Bring foil up and around, sealing edges together but leaving some empty space so that zucchini may cook in its own steam.

Place in a preheated 350° oven, and bake 45 to 50 minutes.

Serves 4.

Note: Any of the squash family can be baked in the same way, as can thinly sliced carrots, green peas, or beans.

STEAMED ZUCCHINI ITALIAN STYLE

¼ cup water
Salt
  4 medium zucchini, trimmed and
    thinly sliced
  1 clove garlic, peeled

1 tablespoon olive oil (substitute
    butter if preferred)
¼ cup fine dry bread crumbs
¼ cup freshly grated Parmesan
    cheese*
Freshly ground black pepper

---

* The few seconds it takes to grate your own Parmesan cheese is well worth the effort. The imported Italian variety—purchased in an Italian grocery or at a gourmet-style cheese shop—is so far superior in flavor over its domestic "already-grated-in-the-bottle" American cousin that the two bear little resemblance.

Bring water to boil, and sprinkle lightly with salt. Add zucchini and garlic. Cover and steam until zucchini is crisp-tender. Remove garlic. Drain. Add olive oil, stir to blend, then stir in bread crumbs and cheese. Correct seasoning with additional salt as needed, and add pepper to taste.
Serves 4 to 6.

STEAMED EGGPLANT WITH TOMATO SAUCE

3 ½-inch-thick slices French bread
Butter at room temperature
Parmesan cheese
1 large eggplant
¼ cup Chicken Stock (pages 23–24)

Salt
½ cup tomato sauce (canned or Quick and Easy Creole Tomato Sauce [page 113])
1 small white onion, minced
Freshly ground black pepper

Cut bread slices into bite-size cubes, spread with butter, and sprinkle with Parmesan cheese. Place on foil in a preheated 250° oven until crisp and lightly browned. Set aside.
Peel the eggplant, and cut it into ½-inch slices. Cut the slices into bite-size cubes.
Place chicken stock in a saucepan, and bring to boil. Season lightly with salt. Add the eggplant cubes. Cover and steam until just tender, 4 to 5 minutes. Add the tomato sauce and onion, and cook, stirring often, 2 to 3 minutes more. Add the toasted bread cubes, and cook a final half minute. Correct seasoning with salt and pepper, and if desired, sprinkle with additional Parmesan cheese.
Serves 6.

The flour-butter ball in the following recipe is frequently used in French kitchens. It's called a *beurre manié*, and it does indeed prove that the French know a bit more than they would have you think about short-cut cooking methods. Anytime you want to quickly thicken a sauce or soup, simply knead together 2 parts butter to 1 part flour—in other words make a *beurre manié*—and stir it into the hot but not boiling liquid. *Voilà!* In no time at all it's as thick and creamy as if cooked for hours.

STEAMED BRUSSELS SPROUTS IN CREAM SAUCE

1 tablespoon butter at room temperature
2 teaspoons flour
1 quart brussels sprouts
4 cups water
1 tablespoon salt
1 egg yolk

½ cup light cream
1 cup Chicken Stock (pages 23–24)
½ teaspoon salt
Dash grated nutmeg
White pepper

Cream the butter with the flour, and form it into a small ball. Set aside.

Wash and trim the sprouts. Cover them with the water, add the 1 tablespoon salt, and let soak 20 minutes. Drain.

In a small bowl beat the egg yolk with the cream until blended. Set aside.

Place brussels sprouts in a saucepan, and add ½ cup of the chicken stock and ½ teaspoon salt. Bring to boil, then reduce heat, and simmer for 5 minutes. Cover and steam 10 to 15 minutes or until sprouts are tender. Add remaining stock, and bring to boil. Lower heat, add flour-butter ball, and stir until blended. Add egg yolk and cream mixture, and continue stirring until sauce is thick and smooth. Do not allow to boil after adding cream. Season with nutmeg, pepper, and if needed, additional salt.

Serves 4 to 6.

STEAMED SUCCOTASH SOUTHERN STYLE

¼ pound salt pork
1 tablespoon butter
3 cups fresh lima beans
1 small white onion, chopped
1 small green pepper, seeded and
  chopped

2 tablespoons water
6 ears fresh corn, shucked
Salt
Pepper

Cut the salt pork into quarter-inch dice, and place them in a small saucepan. Cover with cold water, and bring to a boil. Lower heat, and let simmer 4 to 5 minutes. Drain and pat thoroughly dry with paper toweling.*

Place the butter in a large heavy fry pan (one with a tight-fitting cover). Add the salt pork, and cook over medium heat until all fat has been rendered from pork dice and they are crisp. Remove them from the pan with a slotted spoon, and place on paper toweling to drain off excess fat. Reserve.

Add the lima beans, onion, green pepper, and water to the pan. Cover and steam over moderate heat until beans are tender, about 20 minutes.

Grate the kernels from the corncobs, and add them to the bean mixture. Cover pan once more, and steam a final 4 to 5 minutes. Season with salt and pepper, and add the reserved salt-pork dice.

Serves 6.

SWEET AND SOUR CABBAGE

Soggy, overcooked cabbage belongs on nobody's table. Steam only until the raw edge is off, and it will be as light and delicate a vegetable as you are ever likely to serve.

2 tablespoons butter	1 medium tart and crisp apple, peeled, cored, and chopped
1 small head cabbage, coarsely chopped	½ cup (canned) cranberry sauce
2 tablespoons water	1 tablespoon tarragon vinegar
1 small white onion, peeled and chopped	1 teaspoon sugar
	½ teaspoon salt or more if needed

Melt the butter in a large heavy skillet (one with a tight-fitting cover). Add the cabbage and remaining ingredients. Stir to blend. Cover and steam over medium heat until cabbage is crisp-tender. Correct seasoning, and serve.

Serves 4 to 6.

* This step—blanching the salt pork—removes excess salt. It's a good idea to use it in any recipe that calls for this very flavorful but sometimes overpowering meat.

Pureed Vegetables

Are there those people in your house who just won't eat carrots, can't abide spinach or broccoli, and even leave fresh green beans and peas untouched on their plates? Well, try this: Serve these vegetables pureed, and it's very likely you'll see a change of appetite.

BROCCOLI PUREE

1 small bunch of broccoli
(about 1½ pounds)
1 clove garlic, peeled
1 tablespoon butter
¼ cup light cream

Pinch of grated nutmeg
Salt
Freshly ground black pepper
½ cup (approximately) fine dry
bread crumbs

Wash and trim the broccoli, and cut it into small pieces. Place them in a saucepan, and add the garlic and sufficient water to cover. Cook over moderate heat until tender. Drain, and discard garlic.

Place in electric blender. Add butter and cream. Blend until smooth. Do not overblend.

Return mixture to saucepan. Season with nutmeg, salt, and pepper. Add sufficient bread crumbs to bring to the consistency of mashed potatoes, and reheat briefly.

Serves 4 to 6.

PUREE OF GREEN PEAS

2 pounds fresh peas or 1 10-ounce
package frozen peas
¼ cup water
Salt
Freshly ground black pepper
1 clove

3 sprigs parsley
1 bay leaf
2 tablespoons butter at room
temperature
1 tablespoon light cream
⅓ to ½ cup fine dry bread crumbs

Shell the peas, or break the block of frozen peas into several pieces.

Place in saucepan with the water. Season lightly with salt and pepper. Add the clove, parsley, and bay leaf. Cover and cook for 10 to 15 minutes or until the peas are tender. Drain.

Discard clove, parsley, and bay leaf.

Place peas in electric blender, and add butter and cream. Blend until smooth.

Return mixture to saucepan, and add sufficient bread crumbs to bring to the consistency of mashed potatoes. Correct seasoning with additional salt if needed, and reheat briefly.

Serves 4 to 6.

ZUCCHINI AND TOMATO PUREE

3 large or 6 small zucchini
⅓ cup water
2 tablespoons chopped green onions
Salt
Freshly ground black pepper

1 small tomato, peeled, seeded, and chopped
1 tablespoon butter at room temperature
¾ cup (approximately) fine dry bread crumbs

Wash zucchini and chop coarsely. Place in a saucepan with the water and green onion. Sprinkle lightly with salt and pepper. Cover and steam until zucchini is tender. Drain.

Place zucchini in electric blender. Add the tomato and butter. Blend until smooth. Do not overblend.

Return mixture to saucepan. Correct seasoning with additional salt and pepper, and add sufficient bread crumbs to bring to consistency of mashed potatoes. Reheat briefly.

Serves 6.

Braised Vegetables

Braised vegetables (vegetables steamed in butter and stock) have this to recommend them: They need not be rushed to the table as soon as done. They can be kept warm a half hour or so without damage, or they can be prepared ahead and reheated successfully.

Celery, Belgian endive, and cucumbers—usually salad fare—take well to this method of cooking, but so do such winter vegetables as carrots, turnips, and little white onions.

BRAISED ENDIVE

8 heads of endive
Butter
½ cup Chicken Stock (pages 23–24)
1 teaspoon salt

½ teaspoon sugar
2 tablespoons butter, cut in small pieces
2 thin slices imported Swiss cheese

Trim off and discard any discolored leaves from the outside of the endive, and slice away as much of the root as you can without cutting loose the leaves. Place in a heavily buttered baking dish just large enough to hold them.

Combine stock with salt and sugar, and pour over endive. Dot surface with butter. Cover and bake in a preheated 350° oven for 1 hour. Uncover and pour off any remaining liquid.

Cut cheese into strips. Place 1 strip over each endive, and continue to bake until cheese has melted.

Serves 4.

BRAISED CARROTS AND ONIONS

¼ pound fat salt pork, cut in small dice
3 tablespoons butter
12 small white onions, peeled
6 very small young carrots, scraped, or 4 medium carrots, cut in 1-inch pieces

¼ teaspoon salt
¼ teaspoon freshly ground black pepper
1 teaspoon sugar
¼ cup chopped parsley

Place salt pork in a small saucepan. Cover with water, and let simmer over moderate heat for 5 minutes. Drain and pat thoroughly dry with paper toweling.

Melt butter in a heavy skillet, add pork dice, and cook, stirring, over fairly high heat until pork fat has been rendered and dice are crisp. Remove them with a slotted spoon, and drain on paper toweling. Set aside.

Add the onions to the skillet, and cook over moderate heat, turning them with a wooden spoon until they are lightly browned. (They won't brown evenly, but don't let this bother you.) Remove them to a large baking dish or oven casserole.

Add the carrots to the same skillet, and brown them in the same way as the onions. Add them to the same casserole.

Pour the fat from the skillet over the vegetables, and sprinkle them with salt, pepper, and sugar. Cover and bake for 1 hour or until tender.

Transfer with a slotted spoon to the serving dish, add reserved salt-pork dice, and sprinkle with parsley.

Serves 4.

BRAISED CELERY WITH CHEESE SAUCE

6 celery hearts	¾ cup Chicken Stock (pages 23–
2 tablespoons butter	24)
1 tablespoon corn or peanut oil	2 tablespoons dry sherry
½ teaspoon salt	1 tablespoon flour
¼ teaspoon freshly ground black pepper	⅓ cup grated Swiss cheese

Wash celery hearts under cold running water. Pat thoroughly dry with paper toweling. Cut lengthwise in half.

Heat butter and oil in a large heavy skillet (one that can be used in the oven). Add celery hearts, cut side down, and cook over low heat until lightly browned. Turn and lightly brown rounded sides. Sprinkle with salt and pepper. Add stock and sherry.

Cover skillet, place in a preheated 350° oven, and bake 30 to 40 minutes or until celery is tender.

Return skillet to top of stove, and remove celery hearts to a warm serving dish.

Add 2 to 3 tablespoons of the cooking liquid to the flour, and stir to a smooth paste. Add this to the cooking liquid, and stir over low heat until sauce begins to thicken. Add cheese, and continue to cook and stir until cheese melts and sauce is thick and smooth. Pour over celery hearts, and serve.

Serves 6.

Chinese-Style Stir-Fried Vegetables

Almost any vegetable or combination of vegetables may be stir-fried in the Chinese manner, and the results will be simply superb.

Vegetables are cut into paper-thin slices, chopped into cubes that are less than bite size, diced, minced, shredded, or broken into flowerets, and then quickly fried in hot seasoned oil. A little liquid is added, the pan is covered, and steam finishes the cooking process in what seems like no time at all. Nutrition is retained, and though vegetables are thoroughly cooked, they remain flavorful and delightfully crisp. Dry fluffy white rice is their natural accompaniment, but they can be successfully served with such Occidental fare as pasta or potatoes.

Tips for Stir-Frying

Slice vegetables as thinly as possible, or cut them into uniform small dice, or shred them very fine.

Blot all vegetables thoroughly dry before adding to oil.

Always use a large heavy skillet with a tight-fitting cover, preferably one with sloping sides so that vegetables may be easily tossed and stirred.

SWEET AND SOUR CABBAGE, STIR-FRIED CHINESE STYLE

2 tablespoons sesame- or safflower-seed oil
1 clove garlic, peeled and cut in half
½ teaspoon salt
1 medium head cabbage, shredded
1 medium carrot, scraped and finely shredded

½ small green pepper, seeded and finely shredded
3 tablespoons water
1 tablespoon brown sugar
1 tablespoon white-wine vinegar
1 tablespoon soy sauce
Salt
Pepper

Place a large heavy skillet over high heat for a half minute. Add the oil, garlic, and salt. When oil starts to sizzle, remove garlic. Add cabbage, carrot, and green pepper. Cook, stirring and turning vegetables until well coated with oil. Reduce heat to moderate.

Add water, cover skillet, and let steam 2 to 3 minutes or until vegetables are tender but still crisp.

Sprinkle with sugar, vinegar, and soy sauce. Stir to blend, lifting and turning cabbage so that seasoning is evenly distributed. Cover and steam 20 seconds. Correct seasoning with salt and pepper.

Serves 4.

CHINESE STIR-FRIED MIXED VEGETABLES WITH RICE

2 tablespoons sesame- or safflower-seed oil
1 clove garlic, peeled and cut in half
¼ teaspoon salt
1 slice fresh ginger (optional)
2 medium carrots, scraped and cut diagonally at a 45° angle into paper-thin slices
1 medium (purple) onion, peeled and very thinly sliced
1 medium turnip, peeled and very thinly sliced—each slice cut in half
3 tablespoons Chicken Stock (pages 23–24) or water
1 small can bamboo shoots, drained and thinly sliced
½ pound fresh spinach
1 tablespoon soy sauce or more if desired
Pepper
2 cups cooked rice

Place a large heavy skillet over high heat. Add oil, garlic, salt, and ginger. Heat to sizzling. Remove, and discard garlic. Add carrots, onion, and turnip. Cook, stirring and tossing the vegetables until each is well coated with oil.

Add stock, and reduce heat to medium. Cover skillet, and steam 3 to 4 minutes or until vegetables are crisp-tender. Stir occasionally. Add bamboo shoots, spinach, and soy sauce. Sprinkle with pepper, and stir to blend ingredients. Cover once more, and steam for about 1 minute or until spinach is tender. Remove ginger. Correct seasoning with additional salt or soy sauce if desired.

Place cooked rice on a long oval platter. Spoon vegetables in center. Pour sauce over both.

Serve with roast meat (especially good with roast pork), or serve with broiled chops or roast chicken or duck.

Serves 4.

STRING BEANS WITH WATER CHESTNUTS

1 pound fresh green beans, cut
  into 1-inch lengths
2 tablespoons sesame- or
  safflower-seed oil
⅓ teaspoon salt or more as needed
1 clove garlic, peeled and cut in
  half
1 slice fresh ginger (optional)

1 tablespoon dry sherry
½ cup (canned) water chestnuts,
  drained and thinly sliced
¼ cup Chicken Stock (pages 23–
  24)
1 tablespoon soy sauce
Pepper

Plunge beans into boiling water. Boil for 2 minutes. Drain. Pat
thoroughly dry with paper toweling.

Place a heavy skillet over high heat. Add oil, salt, garlic, and ginger.
Heat to sizzling. Remove garlic. Add beans, and cook, stirring, until
they are evenly coated with oil, about 1 minute. Reduce heat to moderate, add sherry, chestnuts, and stock, cover, and let steam until beans are
tender, 4 to 5 minutes. Remove ginger. Add soy sauce, pepper to taste,
and additional salt if needed.

Serves 4.

SNOW PEAS AND MUSHROOMS
(Dieter's Delight)

1 10-ounce package frozen snow
  peas
2 tablespoons sesame- or
  safflower-seed oil
Salt

1 pound fresh mushrooms,
  trimmed and diagonally sliced
1 tablespoon soy sauce
Pepper

Remove snow peas from package, and let thaw at room temperature,
about 15 minutes. Pat thoroughly dry.

Place a heavy skillet over high heat. Add oil and ⅓ teaspoon salt.
When oil starts to sizzle, add mushrooms and snow peas. Stir-fry until
each vegetable is coated with oil. Reduce heat to moderate. Cover skillet,
and let steam 2 to 3 minutes, stirring occasionally. Season with soy sauce
and pepper. Correct seasoning with salt.

Serves 4.

Baked Vegetables

A baked vegetable is especially nice as the one hot dish for a buffet supper that features cold baked ham or turkey plus a good salad of all sorts of mixed greens.

BAKED SPINACH PUDDING

12 large soda crackers
½ pound fresh spinach
3 egg yolks, beaten
½ pound ricotta cheese or pot cheese
2 tablespoons heavy cream or sour cream

¼ teaspoon salt
¼ teaspoon pepper
3 egg whites
2 tablespoons grated Parmesan cheese
2 tablespoons melted butter

Crumble 10 of the soda crackers into a large mixing bowl. Make fine crumbs of remaining crackers (in electric blender or with rolling pin).

Chop spinach, and place in a colander. Wash thoroughly under cold running water. Place—with only the water that clings to the leaves—in a large saucepan over medium heat. Cover and cook 5 to 8 minutes or until wilted but still bright green in color. Add with cooking liquid to soda crackers in mixing bowl. Cool slightly. Add egg yolks, cheese, cream, and salt and pepper. Blend well. (*The dish can be made ahead to this point.*)

Beat egg whites until stiff, and gently fold into spinach mixture.

Pour into a lightly greased square baking pan or a soufflé dish.

Sprinkle with the fine cracker crumbs, Parmesan cheese, and butter.

Place in a preheated 350° oven, and bake 30 to 45 minutes or until firm.

Serves 6.

BAKED ZUCCHINI CUSTARD

Here is another dish that can be made ahead, then put in the oven about 30 minutes before the meal is to be served. You might team up this hearty dish with Carrots Vichy (page 88) and steamed green beans for a very good all-vegetable lunch.

2 slices white bread
4 medium zucchini, trimmed
1 small white onion, peeled
1 medium tomato
1 tablespoon oil
1 tablespoon water

¼ teaspoon salt
¼ teaspoon freshly ground black pepper
½ teaspoon sugar
2 eggs, lightly beaten
¼ cup grated Parmesan cheese

Place bread in a 350° oven, and bake until dry and crisp. Break up into large crumbs.

Chop fine the zucchini and onion.

Cut tomato in half, then gently squeeze each half to remove seeds. Coarsely chop.

Place zucchini, onion, and tomato in a large saucepan, and add oil, water, salt, pepper, and sugar. Cover and cook over low heat until vegetables are very tender, about 30 minutes.

Remove from heat, and mash still-solid vegetables into vegetable liquid. Add bread crumbs, and blend until mixture is fairly smooth. Add eggs and grated cheese. Mix well.

Transfer to a shallow baking dish or to individual ramekins. (*Can be made ahead to this point. Cover and refrigerate until ready to bake.*) Place in a preheated 325° oven, and bake until firm, about 30 minutes.

Serves 6.

BAKED STUFFED TOMATOES

This dish is very *haute cuisine,* but it is easy to prepare, and when baked on foil, no pans to wash!

4 medium tomatoes
Salt
¾ cup fine dry bread crumbs, made from French or Italian bread
¼ cup grated Romano cheese
1 small white onion, peeled and very finely minced

½ teaspoon salt
⅛ teaspoon paprika
⅛ teaspoon cayenne pepper
3 tablespoons butter, melted and cooled
1 tablespoon cold butter slivers

Cut tomatoes in half. Holding each tomato half cut side down, squeeze gently to remove seeds and liquid. With the handle of a small teaspoon scoop out any seeds that resist, removing as little of the sectional walls as possible. Sprinkle insides lightly with salt, and place cut sides down on waxed paper to drain still further for 8 to 10 minutes.

Combine bread crumbs with all remaining ingredients except butter slivers, and stuff tomato halves with mixture. Dot with slivers of butter, and place on a double-thick sheet of lightly greased foil. Bake in a preheated 350° oven for 25 to 30 minutes or until soft but not falling apart.

Makes 8 stuffed tomato halves.

CORN SOUFFLÉ

¼ cup butter
1 small white onion, peeled and chopped
1½ cups fresh corn, cut off the cob (4 or 5 ears)
3 eggs, separated
1 teaspoon salt

¼ teaspoon dry mustard
½ teaspoon sugar
¼ teaspoon freshly ground black pepper
½ cup crumbled sharp cheddar cheese

Melt the butter in a heavy skillet over moderate heat. Add the onion, and cook, stirring, until transparent. Add the corn, and continue to cook and stir 2 to 3 minutes. Remove from heat and cool.

Beat the egg yolks until light and "lemony." Add salt, mustard, sugar, pepper, and cooled corn mixture.

Beat the egg whites until stiff but not dry. With a "light hand" quickly stir in about ¼ of the corn mixture, then gently fold into the corn mixture.

Pour into a well-greased 2-quart soufflé mold. Place mold in a pan of warm water, and bake in a preheated 350° oven for 1 hour—until soufflé is firm to the touch and lightly browned.

Serve at once.

Serves 4.

8

Sauces and Savory Butters

Contrary to popular opinion, great sauces do not require special skill to prepare, and, more often than not, they can be made in a matter of minutes. A little knowledge is all that is needed, and that knowledge is easily obtained.

Learn the simple secrets of preparing a classic brown sauce, and you immediately have the know-how for superb meat sauces beyond numbering. Acquire skill in making an easy but perfect white sauce, and there at the tip of your saucepan is the base for a hundred more glorious creamy dishes. Add a good well-seasoned tomato sauce to your repertoire, become acquainted with the chemistry of sour-cream sauces, then master the child's play of butter sauces, and you have it!

Brown Sauce

Classic brown sauce is listed in French cookbooks as *sauce espagnole*, but despite its name, nothing could be more French. In both France and the United States it is the basic sauce for meat. It is also one of the great foundation sauces—the basis of a variety of other very French, very good sauces that are actually quick and easy to make.

Though many American cookbooks of the so-called convenience school of cooking blatantly state that canned beef gravy serves as an admirable substitute for brown sauce made at home, for the sake of your sauce, don't you believe them. Though canned gravy can indeed substitute for homemade, the resulting dish will be inferior.

103

Here is a quick and easy version made "special" with homemade stock (Chapter 3).

BROWN SAUCE

2 tablespoons butter or beef drippings	1 tablespoon tomato puree
2 tablespoons flour	⅛ teaspoon thyme
2 cups Beef Stock (pages 22–23)	⅛ teaspoon marjoram
1 bay leaf	Salt
	Freshly ground black pepper

Melt the butter (or heat the beef drippings) in a heavy saucepan over low heat. Remove pan from heat, and stir in the flour. When blended, cook, stirring, over the lowest possible heat until mixture is light brown in color.

Slowly add the stock, stirring as it is added. Increase heat, and bring to a boil, stirring constantly with a wire whisk.

Again reduce heat to very low, and add bay leaf, tomato puree, thyme, and marjoram. Cook, stirring often, until sauce is thick and smooth. Season to taste with salt and freshly ground black pepper. Remove bay leaf.

Makes about 1½ cups sauce.

Serve with any meat, or use as a base for other sauces.

If desired, double the recipe, and freeze what you do not use. Brown sauces freeze well and can be successfully kept in the freezer compartment of your refrigerator. Use within 1 month.

Freeze in ice-cube trays. When frozen, eject cubes, and place in plastic bags, seal, and store in freezer.

One frozen cube is equivalent to approximately 2 tablespoons liquid sauce.

Variations on the Brown-Sauce Theme

SAUCE PIQUANT

Blend 2 tablespoons Dijon mustard with 1 tablespoon Worcestershire sauce, and stir in ¼ cup dry white wine. Add mixture to 1½ cups brown sauce, and cook, stirring, 2 to 3 minutes.

This is especially good with broiled chops or roast beef.

MADEIRA SAUCE

Add ¼ cup Madeira to 1½ cups brown sauce, and cook, stirring, 2 to 3 minutes. Stir in 1 tablespoon Cognac or other good brandy and 1 tablespoon butter. Cook and stir until butter dissolves. Correct seasoning with salt and pepper.

Serve with veal, with steak, or with other beef dishes. Elegant with *filet mignon*.

MUSHROOM SAUCE

Add one 3- or 4-ounce can sautéed-in-butter mushrooms and ½ cup dry white wine to 1½ cups brown sauce. Stir in 1 teaspoon Dijon mustard. Heat thoroughly.

Serve with veal, lamb, or beef. Try this one over hamburger steaks.

SAUCE DIABLE

Sauté 2 tablespoons minced shallots in 1 tablespoon butter until soft. Add 1½ cups brown sauce, 2 tablespoons Cognac or other good brandy, and 1 tablespoon (bottled) Escoffier Sauce Diable. (You may substitute any good steak sauce.)

Serve with beef, lamb, or veal.

SAUCE ROBERT

Sauté 2 tablespoons minced green onion in 1 tablespoon butter until soft. Add 2 tablespoons white-wine vinegar, and stir until vinegar has reduced to half. Add 1½ cups brown sauce. Stir in 1 tablespoon (bottled) Escoffier Sauce Robert. Heat thoroughly.

This is great with lamb.

SAUCE ITALIENNE

Sauté 2 small chopped tomatoes in 2 tablespoons butter until very soft. Add one 3- or 4-ounce can chopped mushrooms, 2 tablespoons tomato paste, and 1½ cups brown sauce. Add 3 or 4 dashes of Tabasco sauce and ¼ cup Chianti or other good dry red wine. If desired, add 1 or

2 chopped spicy Italian sausages. Cook, stirring often, over low heat for 10 to 15 minutes.

Serve over veal, lamb, or beef. Perfect for sautéed veal scallops. Good, too, over pasta of any kind.

ONION SAUCE

Peel and chop 2 small white onions. Place in electric blender with ¼ cup Cognac or other good brandy. Blend until smooth. Add to 1½ cups brown sauce. Cook, stirring, until well heated.

Serve with steak or chops.

White Sauce

White sauce, cream sauce, béchamel, or velouté—the names are different, but these sauces are basically the same. Béchamel is made with milk, velouté calls for stock, while white and cream sauces can be democratically prepared with either milk, cream, stock, or a combination of all three.

In all recipes butter is melted, flour is added, and the mixture is cooked and stirred to what is known as a white roux. Liquid comes next, seasoning is added, then the sauce is cooked until thick and smooth. Simple? Of course, but there are tricks to the trade.

The butter should be melted over very low heat. It must never, but never, sizzle or brown. The flour should be sprinkled evenly over the butter, and the mixture should not just be blended but cooked, without browning, for no less than a full minute, or the final results will taste floury and raw. Liquid is added slowly, blended as it is added smoothly into the roux. Then the sauce is cooked—again slowly—until as thick as required for the particular dish in which it is to be used. It sounds time-consuming, but it's not. The entire process takes only a few minutes' work.

THIN WHITE SAUCE

1 tablespoon butter	1 cup liquid
1 tablespoon flour	Salt and white pepper to taste

MEDIUM WHITE SAUCE

2 tablespoons butter	1 cup liquid
2 tablespoons flour	Salt and white pepper to taste

THICK WHITE SAUCE

3 tablespoons butter	1¼ cups liquid
3 tablespoons flour	Salt and white pepper to taste

There are many possible liquids you can use. Here are a few: milk; half milk, half cream; veal, chicken, or fish stock; part stock, part milk; three-fourths milk, one-fourth dry white wine, sherry, or vermouth; one-half milk, one-fourth stock, one-fourth wine, vermouth, sherry, Cognac, or brandy.

To make a white sauce interesting you may add slivered almonds, slivered (canned) water chestnuts, Italian pignolias (pine nuts), or chopped walnuts or pecans. Also good are sliced fresh or canned mushrooms, ripe-olive slivers, strips of pimiento, minced parsley, finely chopped chives or green onion, peeled and chopped cucumbers, or chopped hard-cooked egg. Then there's cheese—not just American, though. Try grated Swiss or crumbled cheddar as well as crumbled Roquefort or blue. As to seasoning, after pepper and salt you might consider a dash or more of paprika, nutmeg or ginger, curry powder, or just a bit of prepared horseradish, mustard, or tomato puree.

Variations on the White-Sauce Theme

RICH CREAM SAUCE

3 tablespoons butter	¾ cup light cream
3 tablespoons flour	Salt
1 cup Chicken Stock (pages 23–24)	White pepper
	1 tablespoon lemon juice
3 egg yolks	1 tablespoon chopped parsley

Place the butter in a saucepan over low heat. When melted, stir in the flour, and blend until smooth. Slowly add the stock, stirring as it is added. Remove from heat.

Beat the egg yolks into the cream, and slowly pour this into the first mixture, beating with a wire whisk as it is added. Return pan to low heat, and cook, stirring, until sauce is thick and smooth. Season to taste with salt and pepper. Remove pan from heat. Stir in lemon juice and parsley. Serve at once.

Makes about 2 cups sauce.

CREAM SAUCE FOR FISH

2 tablespoons flour	2 egg yolks, lightly beaten
2 tablespoons butter	Salt
1 8-ounce jar clam juice	Pepper
1 cup cream	

Melt the butter in a heavy saucepan over low heat. When bubbly, stir in the flour, and cook, stirring, until well blended. Remove pan from heat, and slowly add clam juice, stirring as it is added. Return pan to heat, and continue to cook and stir until sauce thickens. Combine cream and egg yolks, and beat until blended. Add 2 to 3 tablespoons of the hot sauce, and blend quickly. Pour this mixture into hot sauce, and cook, stirring, until thick and smooth. Season to taste with salt and pepper.

Serve over any baked or broiled or poached fish. To make special, just before serving you may add ¼ to ½ cup chopped cooked shrimp or lobster or flaked crabmeat. Or try ½ cup tomato puree or ½ cup grated Swiss cheese or curry to taste.

Makes about 2 cups sauce.

OYSTER AND CLAM SAUCES

Substitute ½ cup oyster liquid for clam juice in preceding recipe. Add ½ cup chopped oysters just before serving. For clam sauce add ½ cup chopped clams just before serving.

SOUR-CREAM WHITE SAUCE

2 tablespoons butter	½ cup sour cream
1 tablespoon flour	1 tablespoon lemon juice
¾ cup Chicken Stock (pages 23–24)	Salt
	Paprika

Melt the butter in a saucepan over low heat. Stir in the flour, blend well, and cook over very low heat for 2 to 3 minutes. Slowly add the chicken stock, stirring as it is added. Cook and stir until thick and smooth. Add sour cream, stir in lemon juice, and season lightly with salt. Continue to cook, stirring constantly, only until sauce is steamy hot. Stir in paprika. Do not allow to boil after adding sour cream.

Serve with baked, broiled, or poached chicken, or stir into just-cooked steamy-hot broccoli or spinach or over brussels sprouts or asparagus.

Makes about 1¼ cups sauce.

SOUR-CREAM MUSHROOM SAUCE

4 tablespoons butter
1 small onion, peeled and chopped
1 tablespoon flour
½ cup milk
½ cup Beef or Chicken Stock (pages 22–24)

½ pound chopped fresh mushrooms
¾ cup sour cream
Salt
Freshly ground black pepper
Paprika

Melt butter in a large saucepan. Add onion, and sauté over low heat until soft. Sprinkle with flour, and cook, stirring, 1 minute. Pour in milk, stirring as it is added. When smooth, add stock, and continue to cook 2 minutes longer. Add mushrooms, cover, and let simmer 5 minutes, stirring occasionally. Stir in sour cream, and season lightly with salt, pepper, and paprika. Cook, stirring constantly, until sauce is steamy hot. Do not allow to boil after adding sour cream.

Serve as an accompaniment to pot roast or with any roasted or broiled meat.

Makes about 2¼ cups sauce.

ELEGANT SOUR-CREAM HORSERADISH SAUCE

This is milder than the usual horseradish sauce, and it's smooth and creamy.

1 3-ounce package cream cheese at room temperature
1 cup sour cream
2 tablespoons horseradish
½ teaspoon salt
½ teaspoon sugar
2 or 3 dashes Tabasco sauce
2 tablespoons minced chives

Combine ingredients, and blend well. Refrigerate until chilled. Serve with cold boiled shrimp, with lobster, or as an accompaniment to cold roast beef, veal, or lamb.

Makes about 1½ cups sauce.

COLD SOUR-CREAM DILL SAUCE WITH CUCUMBER

1 cup sour cream
¼ cup chopped fresh dill
Salt
1 large cucumber, peeled and chopped

Place sour cream and dill in electric blender, and blend until smooth. Season lightly with salt. Pour into serving bowl, and add chopped cucumber. Chill well.

Serve with poached fish, or mix with crisp salad greens, chilled green beans, or sliced cold beets.

Makes about 1½ cups sauce.

HOT SOUR-CREAM DILL SAUCE

2 tablespoons butter
1 tablespoon flour
¾ cup Chicken Stock (pages 23–24)
4 tablespoons chopped fresh dill or 1 teaspoon dill weed
1 tablespoon white-wine vinegar
1 tablespoon brown sugar
½ teaspoon salt
1 egg yolk, lightly beaten
¾ cup sour cream

Melt butter in a saucepan over low heat. Add flour, and stir until smooth. Cook, stirring, 3 minutes. Slowly add stock, stirring as it is added. Cook, stirring, until sauce begins to thicken. Add dill, vinegar, sugar, and salt. Remove from heat.

Combine egg and sour cream. Blend well, then slowly add to sauce, stirring rapidly as it is added. Return pan to heat, and cook, stirring, until sauce is smooth and thick. Do not allow to boil after adding sour cream.

Serve over boiled potatoes, with vegetables, with any fish, or on poached eggs over slices of baked ham on toast. This last is just lovely.

Makes about 1½ cups sauce.

GREEK AVGOLEMONO SAUCE

Here is a tart and creamy lemon and egg sauce as versatile as it is quick and easy to prepare. In Greek kitchens a dozen or more versions are used as an ingredient in fish and meat dishes, vegetables, soups, and stews. Use with American food as a sauce for broiled fish, stir into just-cooked and well-drained hot vegetables, or serve as an accompanying sauce to roast lamb or broiled lamb chops.

2 tablespoons flour	¼ teaspoon salt
2 tablespoons lemon juice	⅛ teaspoon white pepper
3 egg yolks	1 tablespoon finely chopped
1½ cups Chicken Stock (pages 23–24)	parsley

Combine flour and lemon juice, and mix to a smooth paste. Add egg yolks, and beat until well blended and light.

In a saucepan bring stock to a full boil. Remove from heat.

Slowly add about ¾ cup of the hot stock to the egg-yolk mixture, beating with a wire whisk as it is added. Slowly pour this mixture into the hot stock, again beating with a whisk as it is added. Season with salt and pepper.

Return pan to low heat, and cook, stirring with a whisk, until sauce thickens to the consistency of thick cream. Stir in the parsley.

Makes about 2 cups sauce.

Note: Sauce may be kept warm over hot water for 20 to 30 minutes.

EGG SAUCE

Simple, delicious, quick to make, and lighter than conventional cream sauce for dressing steamed vegetables is Egg Sauce.

¾ cup cream	Salt
2 hard-cooked eggs	White pepper
Pinch (or more) curry powder	

Heat the cream in the top half of a double boiler over simmering water.

Mash the yolks of the hard-cooked eggs. Add 2 to 3 tablespoons of the hot cream, and mix to a paste. Add mixture to the hot cream, and blend well.

Season with curry powder, salt, and pepper. Chop the egg whites, add them to the sauce, and ladle immediately over just-cooked steamy-hot vegetables.

Makes about 1 cup sauce.

Beautiful Red Tomato Sauces

A good tomato sauce must simmer for hours, says the old cookbook. Not so. Here's a made-in-minutes tomato sauce that will do you proud.

Take 4 large ripe and juicy tomatoes. Chop and chop. Put them and their juice in a saucepan over low heat without adding anything else. Let the tomatoes cook, chopping them still further with the tip of a spatula until a sauce is achieved. Now remove them from the heat, and add a lump (1 tablespoon) of butter, stirring until it disappears. Season with salt and freshly ground black pepper; add a large dash of Tabasco sauce and about ½ cup minced parsley. When mixed with servings of just-cooked spaghetti and topped with grated Parmesan cheese, you have a very Italian dish.

Makes about 1 cup sauce.

QUICK AND EASY CREOLE TOMATO SAUCE

2 tablespoons olive oil
1 large onion, peeled and
  chopped
1 clove garlic, peeled and minced
1 small green pepper, seeded and
  chopped
1 celery stalk, chopped
1 1-pound 3-ounce can tomatoes
1 3-ounce can tomato puree
1 cup water

1 teaspoon salt
½ teaspoon freshly ground black
  pepper
⅛ teaspoon thyme
¼ teaspoon oregano
1 tablespoon sugar
2 or 3 drops Tabasco sauce
1 teaspoon flour
¼ cup sherry

Heat oil in a heavy skillet. Add onion, garlic, green pepper, and celery. Cook, stirring, until vegetables are limp. Add tomatoes, tomato puree, and water. Season with salt, pepper, thyme, oregano, sugar, and Tabasco. Let simmer over low heat for 1 to 1½ hours.

Blend flour to a paste with a little of the sherry. Add to sauce with remaining sherry. Cook, stirring occasionally, for 10 to 15 minutes. Correct seasoning with additional salt as desired.

Serve with meats or pasta.

Makes about 3 cups sauce.

SPICY TOMATO SAUCE

2 tablespoons butter
1 medium onion, peeled and
  chopped
½ small green pepper, seeded and
  chopped
1 celery stalk, chopped
2 medium tomatoes, seeded and
  chopped

1 bay leaf
2 or 3 dashes Tabasco sauce
¼ teaspoon basil
Salt
Freshly ground black pepper
1 cup (bottled) catsup

Melt butter in a saucepan over low heat. Add onion, green pepper, and celery. Sauté until vegetables are limp. Add tomatoes, bay leaf,

Tabasco sauce, and basil. Sprinkle lightly with salt and pepper. Blend and let simmer over very low heat for 30 to 45 minutes. Remove bay leaf. Add catsup, and continue to cook until sauce is steamy hot. Correct seasoning with additional salt and pepper.

Serve with boiled beef tongue, with lamb, or over pasta.

Makes about 2 cups sauce.

Tart Sauces, Hot and Cold

Here's a sauce to serve with any fish, whether fried, baked, broiled, or poached.

SPICY FISH SAUCE

3 tablespoons butter
¾ cup (bottled) catsup
2 tablespoons white-wine vinegar

1 teaspoon prepared mustard
1 tablespoon prepared horseradish

Melt butter in a small skillet. Add catsup, vinegar, and mustard. Cook, stirring, over medium heat until bubbly. Stir in horseradish, and remove from heat. Ladle over cooked fish on serving plates, or pour into a sauceboat, and pass at the table.

Makes about ¾ cup sauce.

RIVERBOAT TARTAR SAUCE FOR FRIED FISH

½ cup mayonnaise
1 tablespoon prepared mustard
¼ cup (bottled) catsup
2 tablespoons grated onion

¼ cup chopped sweet mixed pickle
1 teaspoon Worcestershire sauce
Dash Tabasco sauce

Blend all ingredients, and mix well. Chill 1 hour or longer before serving.

Makes about 2 cups sauce.

TWO-MINUTE MUSTARD SAUCE
for Hot or Cold Vegetables

½ cup oil
3 tablespoons tarragon vinegar
½ teaspoon salt

¼ teaspoon freshly ground black
  pepper
1 teaspoon grated onion
1 tablespoon Dijon mustard

Combine all ingredients, and beat with a wire whisk until well blended. Pour over just-cooked hot vegetables. Serve hot.

Or pour over just-cooked hot vegetables, and refrigerate until well chilled. Pour off excess dressing, and serve on lettuce as a first-course salad.

Makes about ¾ cup sauce.

EASY APPLE-MINT SAUCE
for Lamb or Boiled Beef

1 cup unsweetened applesauce
1 8-ounce jar mint jelly

1 tablespoon prepared
  horseradish

Heat the applesauce in a heavy skillet. Add the jelly, and cook, stirring often, over low heat until melted. Remove from heat, and stir in horseradish.

Serve hot or cold.

Makes about 2 cups sauce.

Savory Butters

These sauces are used by professional chefs to add special flavor to short-order foods—grilled steaks, chops, and fish. They can be made ahead and stored in your freezer for quick use whenever a good sauce is what the dish wants.

HERB SAUCE
for Broiled or Sautéed Fish

½ cup (1 stick) butter at room
   temperature
1 tablespoon lemon juice
1 tablespoon fresh minced
   parsley

1 tablespoon fresh minced or 1
   teaspoon dried tarragon, basil,
   thyme, or marjoram
Salt to taste
White pepper to taste

Cream the butter, and beat in the remaining ingredients. Refrigerate if desired, but bring to room temperature before using. Spread on any broiled, sautéed, or poached fish just before serving.

MAÎTRE D'HÔTEL BUTTER
for Steak or Chops

½ cup (1 stick) butter at room
   temperature
1 tablespoon Worcestershire
   sauce

1 tablespoon lemon juice
1 tablespoon minced chives
Salt
Freshly ground black pepper

Cream the butter, and beat in remaining ingredients. Spread at room temperature over sizzling hot steak or chops.

CAPER BUTTER SAUCE
for Vegetables or Fish

½ cup (1 stick) butter at room
   temperature

⅓ cup capers, chopped if large
Freshly ground black pepper

Cream butter, and beat in capers. Season with pepper. Stir into cooked and drained vegetables, or spread on poached or broiled fish.

MEUNIÈRE BUTTER
for Meat, Fish, or Vegetables

½ cup butter
1 tablespoon lemon juice

Salt
Pepper

Place butter in a small saucepan over low heat, and cook until it turns a light brown in color. Stir in lemon juice, and season to taste with salt and pepper.

Just before removing from heat you may add any of the following: slivered almonds, chopped parsley, chopped chives, slivered green or ripe olives, sliced seedless grapes, 1 tablespoon Worcestershire sauce, dash of Tabasco sauce, 2 to 3 teaspoons Escoffier Sauce Robert, or 2 to 3 teaspoons Escoffier Sauce Diable.

CURRIED BUTTER
for Fish, Meat, or Vegetables

½ teaspoon curry powder
½ teaspoon grated onion

4 tablespoons butter at room temperature

Combine ingredients, and blend well. Spread on any fish before or after broiling, spread on just-from-the-broiler steaks or chops, or stir into hot vegetables.

ANCHOVY BUTTER
for Fish, Meat, or Vegetables

1 tablespoon anchovy paste
1 tablespoon lemon juice

4 tablespoons butter at room temperature

Combine ingredients, and blend well. Spread on any fish before or after broiling, spread on just-from-the-broiler steaks or chops, or stir into hot vegetables.

ANCHOVY WATERCRESS BUTTER
for Fish

½ cup (1 stick) butter at room temperature

4 to 6 anchovies, mashed
2 tablespoons chopped watercress

Cream butter with anchovies, and fold in watercress.

ROQUEFORT BUTTER
for Steak

½ cup (1 stick) butter at room temperature

3 ounces Roquefort cheese
3 or 4 dashes Tabasco sauce

Cream butter with Roquefort cheese. Stir in Tabasco sauce.

9

Herbs, Spices, and Garnishes

Herbs and Spices

Herbs and spices add zest to the art of quick cooking. But which should you use? How much should you use? And when should you use them in quickly cooked food?

To begin, herbs and spices are more than just seasonings. They are a culinary philosophy. You should not be conscious of their presence—only aware of the wonderful flavor of the finished dish. If you are unsure of how much is enough, go easy at first. Then use more if it pleases your taste to do so. It's easier to add than subtract.

Start by using ¼ teaspoon dried herbs in a dish that serves 4. But remember when cooking with herbs and spices that the nose and the eye are more important than exact measurements. The strength of dried herbs varies according to the quality of the particular brand and the length of time it has been on your shelf. In general, the greener the herb or the redder the spice, the more likely it will be at its height of flavor.

In made-ahead uncooked and chilled foods, such as herb mayonnaise and pickled shrimp, add dried herbs well in advance of serving. To prevent specks in the finished dish, place herbs in a bit of muslin, and remove before bringing to the table.

Place dried herbs in a mortar, moisten with a bit of oil, milk, water, or dry wine, crush with a pestle, and let stand at room temperature ½ hour before using in any quickly cooked dish.

Tips on Buying and Storing

Buy whole spices such as peppercorns and nutmeg, and grind them just before using. The flavor is very much better than commercially ground.

Always buy the smallest possible bottle or jar of dried herbs, and whether partially used or not used at all, discard and buy "new" every three to four months.

Keep dried herbs in tightly sealed glass jars. Keep them in the refrigerator if possible. If not, keep them on a shelf in the coolest part of your kitchen—well away from the stove.

In preparing quick-cooking food fresh herbs are much, much more desirable than commercially bottled ones. So seek and find when in season, or grow your own.

Freeze fresh herbs (basil, mint, parsley, tarragon, chives, etc.) in quantity when available. It's easy. Just wash, drain, dry well, and cut off tough stems. Pack in plastic bags, seal, and store in freezer. They won't be crisp enough to use in salads or such, but in flavor, they are far superior to dried. To use: Chop while still frozen, and use without thawing.

Your Herb and Spice Shelf

Certain herbs and spices are so right for certain foods: basil for tomato dishes, caraway seeds in coleslaw, cinnamon in apple pie. There are countless others. Here's a quick rundown of most-used herbs and some of the foods they enhance.

Next to salt and pepper on your seasoning shelf there should be these additional seasonings: basil, bay leaf, marjoram, parsley, savory, tarragon, and thyme.

Basil: A must in all tomato dishes. Also great in beans, peas, pasta, tomato soup, and egg dishes. Fresh (you can grow it as a pot plant in your kitchen window), it goes in almost all salads: seafood, potato, cucumber, and of course tomato.

Bay leaf: The heart of la cuisine française, the soul of creole cookery. A foundation flavor for stock. Essential to the French bouquet garni. Use in meat, fish, and poultry dishes, but use sparingly or its flavor will be over-powering.

Marjoram: Enhances cheese dishes, scalloped potatoes, and almost all vegetables from asparagus to zucchini, as well as all salads: potato, vege-table, chicken, or green.

Parsley: The indispensable herb. Chopped as an ingredient in appetizers, soups, sauces, hash, and casserole dishes. In the leaf as a garnish for every conceivable main course, cold or hot.

Savory: Known in Europe as the bean herb. It's the right flavor for all the pea, bean, and lentil family, fresh or dried. Also good in meat loaf, meatballs, and croquettes. Distinctive in salads and has a way with left-overs besides.

Tarragon: One of the classic *fines herbes* of France. The most versa-tile of all herbs. Like the boy who can play most instruments in the band, tarragon can lay ensemble, solo, or take any part. Essential in Béarnaise and tartar sauces. For double-quick cooking it "goes" in egg salad, deviled eggs, omelets, and other egg concoctions. It complements chicken and veal and adds excitement to fish dishes, both hot and cold.

Thyme: A most adaptable herb. Along with bay leaf it is a standby in stock. Use in fish dishes. Good with many vegetables—carrots, peas, and eggplant, to name a few.

Here are some other herbs and some spices to add to your shelf:

Capers: For numerous sauces both hot and cold. Used also in many recipes from France, Spain, Italy, and Greece.

Caraway seed: For cabbage dishes, from coleslaw to sauerkraut. Also good tossed with boiled potatoes and beets. Great, too, in crisp little cookies and in cakes of the pound-cake variety.

Celery seed: Can be used in any recipe calling for fresh celery, either with or as a substitute.

Chili powder: Not just for Mexican-style cookery but also to be used —but sparingly, it's hot!—in tomato dishes and spicy sauces.

Cinnamon: One of the most familiar spices and certainly one of the most powerful in flavor. Famous in cakes, pies, custards, and puddings, but also to be used—lightly does it—as a seasoning for many quick-cooking dishes, as well as for baked, stewed, or poached fresh or dried fruit.

Cloves: An herb for all seasons. A must for good stocks, and great for ham. For hot and cold drinks.

Cumin: For devotees of Mexican foods. Essential for authentic guacamole. Used in many other great Mexican dishes and in those of other Latin American countries. Sprinkle over just-cooked rice or potatoes, and mix lightly into cheese spreads.

Curry powder: A commercial blend of spices: turmeric, cardamom, coriander, saffron, allspice, cassia, and others. To be used in curry dishes —meat, fish, or fowl—of course, but also try a light sprinkling on soups or vegetables, in cream sauces, or as a seasoning for stuffed eggs.

Dill: For pickling, but also adds quick interest to eggs, cheese dips, and poached salmon and other fish dishes.

Ginger, crystallized and preserved: Served as a sweet. Perfect with espresso for an instant dessert. To be chopped and folded into ice cream or whipped cream and used for numerous sauces.

Ginger, ground: Obviously for gingerbread cakes and "snaps" but also, for the adventurous double-quick-time cook, to be lightly sprinkled on broiled fish, rubbed into chicken before baking, and used lightly in sauces. Great teamed with sugar on baked or broiled fruit.

Ginger root: Important in Chinese cuisine. Use sparingly (a half inch or less) in Chinese stir-fried dishes.

Mint: For mint julep, of course, but also for salads and soups and with such vegetables as carrots and peas. Mixed into sherbet, it's the perfect summertime accompaniment to cold meat or as a garnish for fruit salads and cold platters of all kinds.

Nutmeg: Not just a baking spice. The double-quick-time cook buys it whole and grates it—just a bit—into ice cream, sauces, soufflé mixtures, and any cheese dish.

Oregano: Indispensable in Italian, Spanish, and Mexican cookery. Makes "instant Italian" any dish with tomatoes, be it tomato sauce, baked tomato slices, or a tomato casserole.

Poppy seed: On rolls and in pastry, but also in quick cooking to be added to salads, mixed into just-cooked noodles, sprinkled on crisp-cooked vegetables, and stirred lightly into steamy-hot rice.

Saffron: The most expensive of all spices, but well worth the price. A must for authentic paella. Great in easy-to-make pilaf dishes.

Turmeric: Primarily a curry spice and a spice for curries but also, for the adventurous quick-cooking expert, there's turmeric butter: Add ground turmeric to soft butter, and blend well. Spread on fish just before broiling, stir into piping-hot cooked vegetables, use to sauce boiled potatoes, or stir into just-cooked hot rice.

Condiments and Other Flavorings

In my house the following are essential:

Chutney: Major Gray variety. Not just for curry dishes but also to serve with any cold meat or fowl, to use in filled omelets, to stir into plain boiled rice, to add to numerous savory sauces and stews.

Currant Jelly, Apricot Jam, Sauce Melba: For ham glazes, as accompaniments for lamb, veal, and chicken. To make dessert sauce and special desserts.

Escoffier Sauces, Diable and *Robert:* They are expensive but worth the price. Commercially bottled sauce that enhances steak, chops, roast meat, and fowl. To blend with pan juices and serve as a sauce. To add to stews and casserole dishes. To blend with butter as a spread for deluxe sandwiches.

Horseradish: For sauces: cocktail sauce for seafood, sour-cream and horseradish sauce for boiled beef, and a score of others.

Prepared Mustard: From Dijon or Düsseldorf. To give piquancy to sauces and dressings. To blend with butter and use as a sauce. And, of course, for sandwiches, from hot dogs to smorgasbord style.

Soy Sauce: As a seasoning for both Oriental and Occidental foods.

Tabasco Sauce: The most famous hot sauce. Known and used all over the world. You'll find it on restaurant tables from Maine to Texas, from Brussels to Zanzibar. I use it along with pepper in any dish that "wants a lift."

Tomato Catsup: Necessary for cocktail sauces but also as a mild spice and a thickening agent for certain sauces and stews. To add flavor to meat loaf and casserole dishes.

Worcestershire Sauce: The classic bottled steak sauce; as a seasoning in stews, soups, and meat loaf. In numerous casserole dishes. In meat sauces.

Garnishes

Garnishes are essential to quick cooking. They add the necessary finishing touch, pleasing the eye and adding extra flavor and interest to the meal in less than a minute.

Here are some suggestions:

Sprigs of fresh crisp parsley are an obvious garnish—they do dress up a plate. However, if the folks at your hourse leave them ignored on the plate, try something a little different—fry the parsley, and serve it hot. Have it very clean and very dry, and the oil very hot. Drop sprigs into hot fat, and fry for 10 seconds. Drain on paper toweling. Do this the last thing before serving the meal.

Prepare chopped fresh mint mixed with fresh pineapple chunks, sprinkled lightly with powdered sugar and refrigerated overnight. Next day serve as a garnish for any roast meat.

Watercress thoroughly washed, then thoroughly dried, is a perfect garnish for any platter or plate, but it's twice as good if you first dip each sprig in a mild but flavorful French dressing.

Still on green thoughts: Small sweet gherkins split halfway down and salted almonds inserted in them are a different garnish—with corned-beef hash, for instance.

For chicken hash or creamed chicken you might try this: Sauté large pitted black olives in olive oil that has first been heated with a clove or two of garlic—only takes a minute. Serve hot.

For baked ham try seedless raisins and (canned) mandarin orange sections heated in butter. A small mound goes on each plate.

Large fresh mushroom caps sautéed in butter add a luxury note to broiled hamburger patties. If you would have them with the same glossy look as those served in a fine French restaurant, add a little fresh lemon juice to the butter in which they are to be sautéed.

Another luxury garnish is artichoke bottoms (which come in cans or jars) filled with pureed green peas. For 8 servings cook about ⅓ package frozen green peas according to package directions—only a little longer. Don't drain. Mash well, add about 1 tablespoon heavy cream, and season with salt, pepper, and nutmeg (lightly with the nutmeg). Then thicken with sufficient fine bread crumbs to make them as thick as mashed potatoes. Heat 8 artichoke bottoms, in their own liquid, and stuff with mixture.

Then there's braised celery drained and stuffed with boiled carrots that have been mashed with butter and salt and then mixed with chopped pecans. Very colorful these, and they can be made ahead. Sprinkle with slivers of butter, and reheat in a 350° oven. A little water goes first in the bottom of the pan.

Other garnishes to consider:

Pimiento strips. On omelets and scrambled eggs. Over creamed dishes.

Anchovy fillets. On any creamed dish. Crisscrossed over just-broiled steaks.

Canned artichoke hearts. Heat in butter, and serve with sautéed chicken or roast duck or fish dishes of all kinds.

Small (canned) button mushrooms drained and marinated in a garlicky vinaigrette sauce. Great with cold cuts.

Canned pineapple chunks drained and sprinkled with gin—yes, gin— then chilled. To serve with lamb.

Fresh ripe avocado slices sprinkled with lemon juice. Serve at room temperature. For any broiled or baked fish.

Canned water chestnuts thinly sliced over creamed vegetables.

And, of course, there is caviar over any mild creamed dish, and truffle slices over and on just about any meat, fish, fowl, or seafood.

Fruit as a Garnish

As a believer in fruit with meat and poultry I do suggest you try the following recipes for fruit garnishes. They are easy to make, and they do indeed dress up any platter or plate.

PEACHES CARDINAL

4 large ripe peaches
1 cup currant jelly

1 teaspoon almond extract

Plunge peaches into boiling water for a half minute. Hold under cold running water, and slip off the skins. Cut in half, and remove stones.

Melt jelly in a saucepan over low heat. Add almond extract and peach halves. Let simmer a few minutes.

Serve hot or cold with baked ham or roast chicken.

Serves 8.

MINTED PEARS

6 ripe but firm pears
1½ cups sugar
1½ cups water

2 teaspoons essence of pepper-mint
1 teaspoon green food coloring
½ cup chopped fresh mint

Peel pears, cut lengthwise into quarters, and remove core.

Combine sugar and water in a saucepan over medium heat, and stir until sugar has dissolved. Add essence of peppermint and pears. Let simmer until pears are tender but not falling apart. Remove from heat, and stir in food coloring. Cover and refrigerate until well chilled.

Drain pears just before serving, and sprinkle with chopped mint.

This is a joy to behold and a change from the usual prosaic mint sauce for roast lamb.

Serves 6.

PEACH CONSERVE

2 large navel oranges
6 large ripe peaches
3 cups sugar

¼ cup water
¾ cup coarsely chopped walnuts
1 cup diced mixed candied fruit

Grate sufficient rind from oranges to make 2 tablespoons grated rind. Peel and slice oranges, retaining all juice. Cut slices in half.

Plunge peaches into boiling water for 1 minute. Drain, hold under cold running water, and slip off skins. Remove pits, and dice fruit.

Place orange rind, sliced oranges, orange juice, diced peaches, sugar, and water in a large saucepan. Place over low heat, and cook, stirring often, for 40 to 45 minutes. Add walnuts and candied fruit. Continue to cook, stirring, for a final 10 minutes.

Cool and serve with rice pilaf instead of chutney or with cold or hot roast meats, chicken, turkey, or duck.

If refrigerated, cover and use within 1 to 2 weeks.

Makes about 3 cups conserve.

GLAZED APRICOTS

1 1-pound can whole apricots	½ cup brown sugar
⅓ cup juice from apricots	4 tablespoons butter

Place apricots in a heavy skillet, and add remaining ingredients. Cook over low heat, turning the apricots often with a spoon. When well glazed, drain.

Serve hot with chicken or ham.

Serves 6.

BANANAS ROYAL

1 cup sugar	1 teaspoon Angostura bitters
1 cup water	2 or 3 drops red food coloring
⅓ cup crystallized (candied) ginger	4 ripe bananas
	Nutmeg

Place sugar and water in a saucepan over moderate heat. Stir until sugar has dissolved. Add ginger, and let simmer for 15 minutes. Remove from heat, and stir in Angostura bitters and food coloring.

Peel and slice bananas in half lengthwise. Place in a shallow non-metal pan, and pour syrup over them. Sprinkle with nutmeg. Refrigerate until chilled. Drain and serve as an accompaniment to roast duck, chicken, or turkey.

Serves 6.

10

Desserts

There may come a day when desserts go out of fashion, but thank goodness it hasn't arrived yet. Americans in particular still adore desserts. Ask and many will deny it, but just serve a party meal that doesn't end with a sweet, and believe me your guests will be disappointed.

This doesn't mean spending hours in the kitchen preparing some overrich and calorie-laden concoction or rushing out and buying one— far from it. Light, homemade desserts are the in thing, and they need not take more than a few minutes to make.

The sweet things that follow are not low-calorie. In most cases, however, they are less filling and lower in calories than their commercially prepared counterparts, not to mention those heavy pies and over rich cakes that Mother (or was it Grandmother?) used to take hours to bake.

Quick Desserts

Thaw 1 package frozen raspberries until the frozen block can be broken into small chunks. Put them in your electric blender, and blend to a syrup. Strain, then add ¼ cup Grand Marnier liqueur, and pour into a pretty clear-glass pitcher—that's the first part.

Next whip 1 cup heavy cream until stiff, and sweeten with ⅓ cup confectioners sugar. Pile into a silver bowl.

Lastly compose an eye-pleasing compote (about 4 cups) of fresh

129

fruit: strawberries, sliced fresh peaches, melon balls, pineapple sticks, etc.—any and/or all in-season fruit will do nicely.

Bring all to the table to be admired, then spoon fruit into 6 or 8 tall sherbet glasses, top with whipped cream, and pass the pitcher of beautiful red sauce.

Mix together 6 ounces Roquefort cheese, 6 ounces cream cheese, and 2 tablespoons cream. Beat until light and fluffy. Spoon onto 6 dessert plates, and surround with well-drained (canned) guava shells. Serve with unsalted crackers.

Sauté wedges of fresh pineapple in butter until lightly browned. Sprinkle lightly with sugar. Serve hot—4 to 5 for each person—accompanied by a small wedge of nicely ripened room-temperature Camembert cheese.

Slice sufficient bananas and strawberries to make 1 cup of each. Whip ½ pint heavy cream until stiff, and sweeten it with ⅓ cup sugar. Fold the fruit into the cream along with ¼ cup kirsch. Chill. Serve in glass dessert bowls, and pass a platter of from-the-oven Chocolate Cookies (pages 138–139).

Cream 9 ounces of cream cheese with ⅓ cup Strega. Fold in 1 teaspoon grated orange rind. Place in the center of a large round platter. Surround with 2 pints of washed, ripe, and lightly sugared strawberries. Bring to the table. Have small plates nearby, and let guests help themselves.

Fill your prettiest serving bowl with about 4 cups of fresh fruit: sliced bananas, pineapple chunks, peach slices, strawberries, etc. Sprinkle with a little lemon juice so they won't discolor. Now melt 1 cup raspberry jelly, and stir in 1 ounce of Grand Marnier liqueur. Cool a little, then pour over fruit. Refrigerate until chilled and time to serve—with ice cream perhaps, or maybe over plain cake squares with a bit of sweetened whipped cream over each serving.

Ice Cream

Do you know that Americans have the absolutely best commercially made ice cream in the world? Well, it's true, and not even the most dedicated Francophile will deny it. What's more, plain ice cream can be the base for quickly made desserts that are not only easy and good but the best of all festive sweet endings.

TIPSY PEACH-SUNDAE BOWL

1 1-pound can sliced peaches
   with juice
½ cup blended whiskey

Peach ice cream
Chocolate sauce

Drain peaches, reserving liquid, and place them in your best glass serving bowl or a punch bowl. Add ½ cup of the peach juice and ½ cup whiskey. Cover and refrigerate 2 hours or longer.

Drop in 6 scoops of peach ice cream, and spoon (canned) chocolate sauce over each scoop.

Serve at once from the bowl.

Serves 6.

APPLE BOURBON ICE CREAM

1 pint vanilla ice cream
¾ cup (canned) applesauce

2 tablespoons bourbon whiskey

Let ice cream stand at room temperature until soft but not melted. Place in a large mixing bowl, and working quickly, stir in the applesauce and bourbon. Pack into an ice-cube tray or aluminum loaf pan, cover with foil, and place in the freezer until almost refrozen.

Remove from freezer, and stir with a fork. Cover again, and freeze until firm.

Serves 4 to 6.

SOUTH AMERICAN PARFAIT

Fill tall sherbet glasses ⅓ full with vanilla ice cream. Sprinkle lightly with instant coffee. Cover with chopped salted peanuts. Repeat until glasses are full. Spoon a little (bottled) melba sauce over each serving.

Gild this lily with sweetened whipped cream or not, as you prefer. This is so good it's hard to believe it's so easy and quick to make.

ICE CREAM WITH MARRONS

1 quart vanilla ice cream
1 10-ounce bottle of marrons in syrup
1 ounce Cognac or other good brandy

Let ice cream stand at room temperature for a few minutes to soften.

Drain marrons. Combine marron syrup and Cognac. Quickly fold into ice cream. Spoon onto individual plates.

Place marrons in a potato ricer, and press a generous sprinkling over each serving of ice cream.

Serve at once.

Serves 6 to 8.

SOUR-CREAM AND RUM ICE-CREAM PIE

1 quart vanilla ice cream
¼ cup dark Jamaican rum
1 9-inch Cookie-Crumb Crust made with graham crackers (page 134)
½ pint sour cream
2 tablespoons brown sugar

Let ice cream stand at room temperature until soft but not melted. Then quickly stir in rum. Spoon into crumb crust. Mix sour cream with sugar. Spread over ice cream.

Place pie in freezer, and freeze until firm.

Serves 6 to 8.

BLACK-BOTTOM ICE-CREAM PIE

1 pint chocolate ice cream
1 9-inch Cookie-Crumb Crust made with chocolate cookies (page 134)

2 tablespoons Kahlua liqueur
1 quart vanilla ice cream
Chocolate Curls (below)

Spoon chocolate ice cream into crumb crust. Smooth out evenly. Pour Kahlua liqueur over surface. Add vanilla ice cream, piled high. Decorate with chocolate curls. Freeze until time to serve.

Serves 6 to 8.

CHOCOLATE CURLS

Place a square of bittersweet chocolate in a warm place until just slightly softened. Shave with a potato peeler or a small sharp knife. Longer strokes make longer curls.

PEACH-BRANDY AND PECAN ICE-CREAM PIE

½ cup crushed pecans
2 tablespoons butter
1 quart peach ice cream
¼ cup peach brandy

1 9-inch Cookie-Crumb Crust made with vanilla wafers (page 134)
4 ripe peaches
½ cup sugar
½ cup water

Sauté the crushed pecans in butter until they are lightly browned. Cool.

Let ice cream stand at room temperature until soft. Add brandy and sautéed pecans. Blend quickly but well. Spoon into crumb crust. Freeze.

Plunge peaches into boiling water for a half minute. Hold under cold water, and slip off skins. Cut into fairly thin slices. Combine with sugar and water in a small saucepan, and let simmer until soft but not mushy. Cool in syrup. Chill.

Serve wedges of pie with peaches and syrup spooned over.

Serves 6 to 8.

COOKIE-CRUMB CRUST

1½ cups crumbs from graham
crackers, gingersnaps, vanilla
wafers, or crisp chocolate
cookies

¼ pound butter, melted
2 tablespoons confectioners sugar
1 teaspoon flour

Combine ingredients, and blend well. Press firmly into a 9-inch pie plate. Bake in a preheated 300° oven for 8 to 10 minutes. Cool before filling.

Fruit Desserts

Fresh fruit for dessert can be as simple—and good—as crisp apple slices, but it can be even better, for an elegant fruit dessert is so easily made.

These recipes are from my great restaurant collection; nonetheless, all are simple and quick to prepare.

POACHED PEARS IN CARAMEL-CUSTARD SAUCE

1⅓ cups sugar
1 cup water
6 pears
½ cup dry vermouth
½ teaspoon vanilla extract
4 egg yolks

Few grains salt
½ cup scalded cream
½ cup syrup from poached pears
½ cup (canned or bottled) caramel sauce

Combine 1 cup of sugar and the water in a saucepan, and cook, stirring, over medium heat until sugar dissolves. Add vermouth and vanilla extract. Let simmer 8 to 10 minutes.

Peel pears, cut lengthwise into quarters, and remove core. Add to simmering syrup. Cook until tender but still firm enough to hold their shape.

Let cool in the syrup. Chill thoroughly.

To make the custard: Beat the egg yolks until pale and light. Add the remaining ⅓ cup sugar and the salt, scalded cream, and pear syrup.

Place in the top part of a double boiler, and cook, stirring, over simmering water until the mixture thickens and coats the spoon—175° on a candy thermometer. Remove from heat, and cool.

Drain chilled pears, place them in a serving bowl, and pour custard over them. Pour caramel sauce over custard and around pears, and stir it into the custard just enough to give a marbled effect.

Serves 6.

ORANGES ORIENTAL

6 large oranges
1 cup sugar
1 cup water
½ cup finely diced candied ginger

½ teaspoon arrowroot, mixed to a paste with 1 tablespoon water
¼ cup curaçao or orange liqueur

Peel oranges, and divide fruit into sections. Remove seeds from each with a small sharp knife, taking care to keep sections whole.

Place sugar and water in a saucepan, and stir over moderate heat until sugar dissolves. Let simmer for 5 to 8 minutes, then pour over orange sections. Let stand at room temperature 1 to 2 hours.

Remove orange sections from syrup with a slotted spoon, and place them in a serving bowl.

Return syrup to the saucepan, and bring to a full boil. Reduce heat, add candied ginger, and let simmer for about 5 minutes. Stir in arrowroot paste, and stir until sauce thickens slightly. Remove from heat, and add curaçao. Let cool, then pour over orange sections. Cover and refrigerate until well chilled.

For a rare treat serve over chocolate ice cream (or over vanilla, strawberry, or peach ice cream for that matter) or over custard or cake.

Serves 6.

CREOLE BANANAS AND FRESH FIGS FLAMBÉS

In giving this recipe I'll begin at the ending, then give you the preparations, which amount to almost nothing.

The main-course dishes are cleared away, and the coffee service is placed on the table. The stage is set, and here are the props: a chafing dish (or electric skillet), a large bowl of sliced bananas and fresh figs, a small dish with butter and a small bowl of apricot jam, a bottle of best-quality light rum, and a second large bowl—silver, perhaps—filled with vanilla ice cream, sprinkled liberally with macaroon crumbs.

4 tablespoons butter
6 medium bananas, firm but ripe
Lemon or lime juice
6 large purple figs*
3 ounces light rum

½ cup apricot jam
1½ pints vanilla ice cream
¾ to 1 cup soft macaroon
   crumbs

To serve:

Light the burner under the chafing dish (or heat electric skillet to 325°), and add the butter. When melted, add the bananas, which have been sprinkled with lemon or lime juice, and the figs, and stir gently until each piece is well heated and coated with butter.

Mix 2 ounces of the rum into the apricot jam. Add this to the fruit, and continue to stir until jam has melted. Pour remaining rum over surface, and immediately touch with a lighted match.

Serve flaming over scoops of ice cream, sprinkled with macaroon crumbs.

This is a dessert to remember.

Preparation:

Peel the bananas, and cut into thick slices. Sprinkle wtih lemon or lime juice.

Peel figs, and cut each in half. Combine fruit, and refrigerate until ready to serve.

What else to do? Just the macaroon crumbs. You'll need 8 to 10 macaroons. Crush in a blender, or place them between sheets of waxed paper, and roll into crumbs with a rolling pin and a firm hand.

Serves 6.

* If fresh figs are not available, substitute canned figs—well drained.

SANGRÍA COUPÉ

1 orange, peeled and chopped
1 pint strawberries, hulled and sliced
½ pint raspberries, hulled
1 large ripe peach, peeled and chopped
3 or 4 thin orange slices, each cut into 4 wedges
1 tablespoon lemon juice
½ cup sugar
1 ounce orange or other fruit-flavored liqueur
1 ounce Cognac or other good brandy
⅓ cup dry red wine
1 quart vanilla ice cream

Place fruit in a large serving bowl, sprinkle with lemon juice and sugar, add liqueur and Cognac. Blend lightly with a fork. Let stand 3 to 4 hours. Stir occasionally. Remove orange wedges, and set aside. Add wine.

Spoon a little "sauce" and fruit into the bottom of 6 or 8 tall parfait glasses. Cover each with a scoop of ice cream, repeat, and garnish with an orange wedge.

Serves 6 or 8.

DRUNKEN MELON

Melon for dessert isn't news, but it may be to some if you try this.

Cut a circular piece from the top of a large Persian melon, and scoop out the seeds with a silver spoon. Pour into the melon ½ to 1 cup kirsch, brandy, or light rum. Spread the cut-off piece with soft butter, and replace it on the melon (the butter forms a seal). Refrigerate several hours. Tilt and turn the melon once in a while to distribute the flavor throughout.

Slice into wedges, and remove peel.

Serve with scoops of vanilla ice cream.

Serves 4 to 6.

Frozen Desserts

For the "just-home-from-work" cook a dessert from the freezer is the perfect answer. It could have been prepared a day, a week, or a month ahead for half the price of commercially made desserts, and it will be far superior in both nutrition and flavor.

BISCUIT TORTONI

A homemade Italian dinner calls for a homemade Italian dessert.

1 cup very fine dry macaroon crumbs	1 cup heavy cream
⅓ cup Strega liqueur	½ cup confectioners sugar

Place macaroon crumbs in a nonmetal bowl. Pour Strega over them, and let stand 1 hour at room temperature.

Beat cream until stiff. Beat in sugar, then fold in macaroon crumbs.

Spoon into paper cupcake cups, and freeze until firm.

Makes 8 tortoni.

CHOCOLATE COOKIES

¼ pound butter at room temperature	2 cups flour
1 cup sugar	1 teaspoon baking powder
2 eggs	⅛ teaspoon salt
2 squares unsweetened chocolate	¾ cup chopped walnuts
1 teaspoon vanilla extract	Additional flour as needed

Cream butter with sugar. Add eggs, and beat until very smooth.

Place chocolate squares still in their individual wrappers on a small piece of aluminum foil in a 200° oven until melted. Scrape chocolate from wrappers, and add to butter, sugar, and egg mixture. Blend well. Stir in vanilla.

Add flour, about ½ cup at a time, and blend after each addition. Add baking powder and salt. Fold in nuts.

Cover a large double-thick sheet of aluminum foil lightly with flour.

Spoon dough onto center. (Do not wrap.) Place in freezer until firm but not frozen.

Roll dough (still on foil) into a long thin log. Cut in half. Return to freezer, and freeze until very firm. Place each log in a plastic bag. Seal and store in freezer until ready to bake.

Cut as many slices as desired from frozen log. Return log to freezer.

Bake cookies on foil on a cookie sheet in a 350° oven until firm, 8 to 10 minutes.

Makes about 3 dozen small cookies.

FROZEN WHIPPED-CREAM BALLS

1 pint heavy cream
⅓ cup confectioners sugar

½ teaspoon vanilla extract

Whip cream until stiff. Add sugar a little at a time, and continue to beat as it is added. Flavor with vanilla.

Drop whipped cream by spoonfuls onto cookie sheet or onto long strip of heavy-duty foil. Freeze until firm. Store in plastic bag in freezer until ready to use. Balls will not stick together.

Let stand at room temperature 3 to 5 minutes before serving.

Serve over fresh, canned, or stewed fruit or over cake, pie, or custard.

Makes about 2 dozen small balls.

CHEESE PIE GRAND MARNIER

A very posh frozen pie—company fare really—starts with a simple nursery-room crumb crust but goes on to very adult glories.

1½ cups graham-cracker crumbs
2 tablespoons confectioners sugar
⅓ cup melted butter, cooled
3 eggs
3 3-ounce packages cream cheese at room temperature

½ cup sugar
3 tablespoons Grand Marnier liqueur
1 cup commercial sour cream
2 tablespoons brown sugar

Combine 1 cup crumbs with the confectioners sugar and melted butter. Mix thoroughly. Spread and press mixture on buttered sides and bottom of a 9-inch pie pan. Refrigerate until chilled.

Beat eggs slightly, add cream cheese, and blend well. Add sugar gradually, beating after each addition. Blend in 2 tablespoons of the Grand Marnier liqueur. Pour mixture into crumb-lined pan. Place in preheated 350° oven, and bake 20 minutes or until firm.

Combine sour cream, brown sugar, and the remaining 1 tablespoon Grand Marnier. Sprinkle surface with remaining ½ cup crumbs. Spread over cheese layer. Return pie to oven, and bake a final 5 minutes.

Chill before serving.

Serves 8.

Glamour Desserts

If you are timid about attempting the so-called glamour desserts, such as *pots de crème*, chocolate mousse, or a soufflé, don't be. They are almost as easy and quick to prepare as old-fashioned made-from-a-mix custards and pies. They are also less fattening and twice as delicious.

CHOCOLATE MOUSSE

8 egg yolks
½ cup sugar
4 squares (4 ounces) unsweetened chocolate
3 tablespoons water
1 cup heavy cream

8 egg whites
1 tablespoon Grand Marnier liqueur
2 tablespoons candied orange peel, finely chopped

Beat the yolks with the sugar until light and "lemony" in color.

Place chocolate with water in a small saucepan over low heat, and stir until melted and smooth.

In a large saucepan pour a little of the chocolate into the egg-yolk mixture, and stir rapidly to blend, then pour the mixture into the small saucepan. Add ½ cup of cream. Blend well, and cook, stirring, over low heat until custard is thick enough to coat the spoon. Remove saucepan from heat.

In separate bowls beat the egg whites and remaining ½ cup of cream until stiff enough to stand in peaks.

Fold first egg whites, then cream, thoroughly into the custard. Add the liqueur, and fold in the chopped candied orange peel.

Spoon into a large serving bowl. Chill.

Serves 6 to 8.

COLD MARRON SOUFFLÉ

1½ cups heavy cream
 1 8-ounce can sweetened marron puree
 ⅓ cup confectioners sugar
 1 tablespoon unflavored gelatin
 2 tablespoons cold water

¼ cup boiling water
¼ cup Cognac or other good brandy
Whipped cream
Whole marrons in syrup

Whip cream until stiff. Fold in marron puree and confectioners sugar.

Sprinkle gelatin over cold water. When softened, add boiling water, and stir until gelatin has dissolved. Add Cognac.

Fold into whipped-cream mixture, and beat until blended.

Pour into a 1-quart soufflé mold. Refrigerate until set.

Garnish top of soufflé with whipped cream and whole marrons. Serves 8.

POTS DE CRÈME AU CHOCOLAT

2 squares (2 ounces) unsweetened chocolate
1 cup sugar
8 egg yolks (large eggs)

¼ teaspoon arrowroot
1 teaspoon vanilla extract
1 quart milk

Place chocolate squares still in their individual wrappers on a square of aluminum foil in a 200° oven until melted. Cool slightly.

Combine sugar, egg yolks, arrowroot, and vanilla in electric blender. Blend for a half minute. Turn blender to lowest speed, remove top or center disk, and scrape chocolate from wrappers into blender. Blend until smooth. Pour into a large mixing bowl.

Bring milk to a boil. Add to egg-yolk mixture in a slow steady stream, beating constantly with a wire whisk as it is added.

Strain through a fine sieve or several layers of cheesecloth.

Pour into 8 individual *petits pots* (or into individual ovenproof custard cups). Set them in a large pan, and pour enough water around them to come to about ½ of their depth.

Bake in a preheated 375° oven until firm, about 35 minutes.
Chill well before serving.
Serves 8.

DANISH DEEP-DISH APPLE PIE WITH CRUMB CRUST

2 cups sugar
2 quarts apples, peeled, cored, and sliced
½ cup seedless raisins

½ cup chopped walnuts
¼ pound butter, cut into slivers
¾ cup vanilla-wafer crumbs
¼ cup melted butter

Sprinkle 1 cup of the sugar evenly over the bottom of a flameproof casserole. Place over low heat until melted to à light-brown syrup.

Remove from heat, and cover with a layer of apple slices. Sprinkle with a few of the raisins and nuts. Dot with slivers of butter, and cover with a layer of sugar.

Repeat until all ingredients have been used, ending with a layer of apples. Cover with crumbs, and pour melted butter over surface.

Bake in a preheated 350° oven for 45 minutes. Serve warm with cold sweetened whipped cream.

Serves 6 to 8.

VIENNESE MOCHA CREAM CAKE

2 9-inch sponge-cake layers (homemade or from your best bakery)
1 pint heavy cream
⅓ cup sugar

½ cup (canned) chocolate syrup
2 teaspoons instant coffee
1 egg white
½ cup slivered blanched almonds

Cut each cake layer in half horizontally.

Beat the cream until stiff, then gradually beat in the sugar. Add the chocolate syrup, beating as it is added. Beat in the instant coffee.

In a separate bowl beat the egg white until it stands in stiff peaks. Fold gently but thoroughly into the cream.

Put the cake layers together with some of the mixture. Use remainder to cover sides and top of cake. Sprinkle with slivered almonds.

Refrigerate 1 to 2 hours before serving.
Serves 8.

EASY NO-BAKE BLUEBERRY CHEESE CAKE

1 9-inch sponge-cake layer (homemade or from a good bakery)

9 ounces cream cheese at room temperature

1 cup commercial sour cream

2 tablespoons light rum

1 cup brown sugar

2 cups fresh blueberries

Cut sponge-cake layer in half horizontally to make 2 thin layers.

Combine cream cheese, sour cream, rum, and sugar. Blend them, and beat until light and smooth. Fold in 1½ cups of the blueberries.

Place bottom layer of cake in a 9-inch cake pan, and spread with one half of the cream-cheese and berry mixture. Cover with second cake layer, spread with remaining cream-cheese and berry mixture, and garnish with remaining berries.

Cover pan with foil, and place in the refrigerator until well chilled.

To serve, cut in wedges from the pan.

Serves 6 to 8.

Index

148   THE QUICK GOURMET COOKBOOK